FASHION FWD

FASHION FWD

HOW TODAY'S CULTURE SHAPES TOMORROW'S FASHION

MADELINE NIEBANCK

NEW DEGREE PRESS

FASHION FWD

How Today's Culture Shapes Tomorrow's Fashion

ISBN 978-1-64137-134-6 *Paperback*

978-1-64137-135-3 *Ebook*

For Elisabeth, whose beautiful soul gives me so much strength.

CONTENTS

"Fashion is not something that exists in dresses only. Fashion is in the sky, in the street, fashion has to do with ideas, the way we live, what is happening."

—COCO CHANEL

PASSION FOR FASHION

Ugh, I thought.

"What in the world am I wearing?" I croaked to the group huddled around me. But no one responded.

I glanced down at the blue smock. It didn't seem like something my mom or sister would pick out for me. "Dad! Did you pick this outfit?"

Still nothing.

"Guys, seriously. Who the hell dressed me in this?"

* * *

A week earlier, I walked across the stage to receive my diploma from Georgetown University. I wasn't sure how I got accepted and then allowed to graduate, but I did it!

Those four years flew by, but I felt ready to be an adult. I had a great job with a great company lined up. I was to start in August.

I was beyond excited to begin my next chapter in life. There was just this one little thing I needed to do first...

* * *

Brain surgery.

When I was fifteen, I learned I had malformed blood vessels in my brain. The doctor called it an AVM. Apparently, it was something I was born with. Other than causing some pretty nasty migraines, it didn't really affect my quality of life.

But it could.

The way the doctor explained it, I had a fifty-fifty chance that at some point in my life the AVM would bleed (think brain hemorrhage), and if it bled, there was a 10 percent chance I would not survive.

Math was never my strong suit, but I'm pretty sure that's a 5 percent chance of dying in a snap.

In essence, I had a ticking time bomb in my brain and I didn't know if or when it would explode.

What to do? I saw lots of doctors—got a second, third, and fourth opinion. All agreed there were two options, leave it be or have brain surgery, but none could say unequivocally which was the better choice.

We monitored it for a few years, but as I got older, I realized I didn't like the odds of dying at any moment. So I decided to have the surgery the week after I graduated college. I'd have three months to recover, and then I'd be ready to move to Boston and make my mark in the world of technology. I had a plan.

Well, you know what they say about the best laid plans.

* * *

Now wait just a Coco Chanel second, you must be saying.

This book is about fashion. What does all this brain stuff have to do with fashion?

Well you see, ***fashion is my true passion.***

In middle school, I published a fashion magazine. And by published, I mean my parents took me over to Staples to print out some copies. I called it ***Passion for Fashion.*** **It documented the fashion trends most important to twelve-year-old girls.**

Through high school and college, fashion remained an interest, but not a career choice.

My epiphany came in the months following that morning I woke up in the hospital wearing that gaudy blue hospital gown.

* * *

On May 30, 2017, I checked into New York Presbyterian to get some pre-op work done before my brain surgery scheduled for the next day. All standard stuff, said the doctors.

The last thing I remember from that day is complaining to my parents of a terrible headache, worse than any migraine I'd ever suffered.

* * *

When I woke up, I couldn't speak or move or do much of anything.

I later learned that the pre-op procedure caused a blood clot in my brain, which burst, triggering a massive stroke. I was rushed into surgery, and the doctors saved my life. But there were complications. I lost half of my field of vision and was completely paralyzed on my left side.

And just like that, the girl with a plan would be following a very different path than the one she had mapped out.

* * *

Rehab is hard. With a brain that refuses to cooperate and focus, things I once took for granted like walking and lifting my arm became extremely challenging. But I've learned that a traumatic experience like this has a way of putting things into focus.

I needed to exercise my brain, not just my arm and leg. So I decided to write a book. Surprisingly (to me at least), I gravitated to my true passion—fashion.

So with the focus and vigor only a near-death experience can bring, I set out to document my view of the future of fashion. The world is rapidly changing around us and fashion will not be immune to it. But how will fashion be impacted?

That's what this book is about. I researched cultural trends and the evolution of the industry. I interviewed models, influencers, founders, and writers. I got their views, injected my interpretations, and wrote this book.

My hope is it will expose you to different perspectives and force you to rethink the future of the fashion industry.

* * *

Following my near-death experience, I began to really reflect on how I planned to live.

Every single morning since May 30, 2017, I wake up and state my day's affirmations. It usually goes something like this: ***I am so incredibly thankful to be alive and have the chance to work hard and recover. I know there are no shortcuts to recovery, and each obstacle I face in every moment I live presents me with a unique set of circumstances and choices. How I ultimately decide to make the most out of these opportunities influences my outcome.***

My decision to write this book was a selfish one—to kick start my new life of purpose. I hope it can teach readers not just about where I see fashion progressing as an industry,

but also expose readers to the vast possibilities in reclaiming your life.

Don't worry. This book *is* about fashion—but as my reader I want you to know that my passion is poured throughout each word and each page. *And trust me, writing a book while only being able to type with one hand wasn't easy.*

I am so grateful for all the gifts and blessings God has bestowed on me. Having a strong faith grounds me and opens my eyes to a second chance at life and a world of possibilities. Thanks to that wonderful group of people who not only helped me to discover and deepen my passion for fashion—but also to rediscover myself.

—Maddi Niebanck

HOW TO READ THIS BOOK

"Fashion is a form of ugliness so intolerable that we have to alter it every six months."

—OSCAR WILDE

In late 2015, reality star Kylie Jenner released Kylie Lip Kits, her first cosmetics product that was sold directly to consumers online featuring matte liquid lipstick and lip liner combos.1

The response was overwhelming, with more than 150 million of Kylie's Twitter, FB, and Insta followers snapping them up in minutes. And before many of those rabid fans could get one of her signature kits, they sold out.

Historically that would have meant frustrated fans and competitors planning for "next season" to try and add this to their lineup.

But competing brands were ready—and nearly as fast as Kylie's kits sold out, competitors began releasing and promoting their own matte lipsticks, including shades and colors copied from Kylie's line.[1] They could not afford to miss the trend next season in the event it dissipated as quickly as it had begun.

"We used to deal in trends that lasted five to ten years," said Karen Grant, beauty industry analyst at market research firm The NPD Group.[2] "Now, we think it's a long trend if it lasts twenty-four months."

Labels like Gucci, Ralph Lauren, Burberry, and Rag & Bone—all brands that traditionally controlled trend cycles—are now employing new strategies focused on faster-paced production cycles to cater to consumer demands for instant access to new styles.

"Speed is everything right now," said Karin Tracy, the head of fashion, luxury and beauty industries at Facebook[3]. "For luxury brands, whoever is the fastest right now will have competitive advantage, full stop. They need to step out of the comfort zone of perfection, think about how to move fast and build things to let them do so."

Fast-fashion brands like Zara release new collections four to five times faster than a traditional retail brand, according to the apparel consultancy firm Alvanon.[3] Online-only retailers can update their sites daily with new styles and guide the quickening pace of trends. Within the luxury sector, some brands have disregarded the traditional fashion calendar by switching to a see-now-buy-now model allowing consumers to instantly purchase runway looks. Others are adding more collection drops throughout the year.

Change, speed, and innovation are now the name of the game.

* * *

As I set out to discover and explore what was changing about the fashion industry, I was struck by my inability to pin down one thing. The truth was *everything* was changing.

Instead of asking how fashion is changing, I sought to reveal the biggest forces affecting our world today, and how *those* forces change or poise to change fashion.

In this book, we'll explore some of the biggest trends affecting our entire world—and looking at what that means in fashion. Trends including:

1. Artificial Intelligence
2. The move to digital *everything*
3. Sustainability
4. Wearable tech
5. Social media and its influencers
6. Customization of brand experience
7. Shift to younger innovators/influencers
8. Brand/consumer value alignment
9. A transformed online and offline integrated retail experience
10. … and so much more…

I've organized these chapters into bite-sized chunks, allowing you to learn, explore, and choose for yourself where to dive in further. Feel free to jump around and read whatever grabs your interest.

INTRODUCTION

To me, fashion has always been about self-expression and creativity.

This book profiles the unique intersections of the global and cultural shifts in what we wear and how we shop.

I'll share interviews I conducted to learn about what those in the industry perceive to be the major catalysts of change.

Some stories and insights include:

- Peter Carter, cofounder of needlepoint accessories brand Smathers and Branson, highlighting some challenges faced in launching a business

- Alex Batdorf, founder of ZipFit Denim, discussing how she uses style to empower herself and others
- Joshua Sitt, cofounder of streetwear label Madhappy, sharing the brand's goal to foster a community around experience
- Karina Hoyos, general manager of the only Piazza Sempione boutique in the country, talking about how an integrated and personalized retail experience and strong customer service sets brands apart
- American supermodel Maggie Rizer Mehran discussing evolving beauty standards in the industry

It has become increasingly clear that consumers prefer interaction with brands, and many fashion companies are now switching to direct-to-consumer business models all across the value chain. As retail in brick-and-mortar stores declines, brands seek new ways to appeal to customers digitally and through the creation of community. Even things like the time it takes the product to go from design to shelf has quickened, in part due to the rise and increasing accessibility of fast fashion.

Businesses face challenges with data security and in ensuring that consumers' information is kept private. In today's volatile and uncertain economy, the one thing that has become clear is that the future of fashion is in flux. The West is no longer the most important fashion hub, as the focus continues to shift to emerging markets in the East and South.

Fashion itself is on the verge of major disruption in terms of technological advancements and increasing digitalization. Recent advancements in artificial intelligence and increasing access to digital content put forth by brands alters not just the fashion industry but every industry. The ways consumers purchase fashion has changed immensely. Consumers seek authentic interaction with brands and oftentimes can purchase products directly through social media channels.

* * *

If you've come to this book looking for answers, you may be disappointed.

It's really a book of questions, meant to expose the biggest cultural shifts and enlighten readers on their implications for the fashion industry.

Writing this book has not only exposed me to the challenges faced by fashion in terms of innovation but has also increased my awareness of the issues people face in engaging with the industry.

The fragmentation of the fashion industry today has opened up the conversation around change. Whereas before, fashion may have been perceived as a frivolous and superficial pastime for the wealthy, we are beginning to see the dissolution of these barriers to entry, allowing more people to participate and join the conversation. It is clear that if brands don't begin to shift their methodologies to appeal to a diverse and increasingly younger demographic, they will perish.

A recent analysis on the state of the fashion industry by McKinsey Global Fashion Index and *The Business of Fashion* highlight the state of the industry to be uncertain and challenging, yet optimistic[4]. The identity of the consumer is shifting; consumers of fashion today want it all. They want quality, convenience, newness, and experience—all for an affordable price tag. The consumer today is more connected than ever, able to access brand digital content and product information with merely a tap of their iPhones.

Where does this mean our world is headed?

Change, speed and innovation are now the name of the game.

Come along and see what's *truly* in store.

PART 1

SUSTAINABILITY

"Every time you spend money, you're casting a vote for the kind of world you want."

—AUTHOR AND SUSTAINABLE FOOD ADVOCATE ANNA LAPPÉ

WHAT IS SUSTAINABLE FASHION?

Today's consumers care about ethically sourced clothing. But how commonplace is eco-friendly fashion? Do consumers actually care about sustainable fashion or is this just another passing fad?

* * *

To me, sustainable fashion has always conjured images of

compost heaps and recycled water bottles converted into plasticy looking wallets and totes. Not exactly the pinnacle of high fashion. But the sustainable fashion landscape is changing, and it is increasingly common to see stylish, sustainably sourced clothing.

According to the State of Fashion 2018 report by BoF & McKinsey, 66 percent of millennials around the world are willing to spend more on sustainable fashion.[5]

But what is considered sustainable fashion?

To millennial consumers, supporting brands that produce sustainably across the supply chain is important. As a generation raised to fear the dangers of climate change, millennials at the very least have an awareness of the interconnectedness of our world and the need for textile sustainability.

This generation is more aware of the ecological impacts of fashion production. Textile research group Oeko-Tex found that 60 percent of millennials are interested in sustainable clothing while 69 percent of millennials consider labels such as "eco-friendly" or "sustainable" when buying clothes[5].

"While millennials overwhelmingly claim to embrace sustainability and believe they will drive social change, the eco-friendliness of a fashion product may be the least important factor in their purchasing decisions," researchers at the Laboratory Institute for Merchandising said.[6] Millennial consumers are more motivated by price and quality than sustainability. The research study asserts that millennial and Gen Z consumers believe they can drive change in the fashion industry toward more sustainably produced and ethically sourced clothing.[6] The data also proves that factors such as ease of purchase, affordability, and uniqueness of product rank as more important to consumers than sustainability.[6] It is time brands listen to their millennial customers demanding more sustainable options, without sacrificing quality and affordability.

Millennials and Sustainability

Brands that manage to effectively strike a balance between sustainability and price point without sacrificing aesthetic appeal are sure to be the ones that endure. Why not make it easy for customers and give them the quick and easily digestible sustainability information they need to make purchasing decisions?

Reformation is a sustainable women's clothing and accessories company that practices complete transparency, posting their CO_2 and waste savings on their website. For every product! Reformation is proud of its environmentally friendly habits, and other companies are taking notice. News publication *The*

Week dubbed Reformation's persimmon floral midi dress "the perfect sustainable fashion choice for spring."[7]

* * *

Many fashion brands promote themselves as socially conscious, eco-friendly companies, and the industry is headed toward a more holistic approach to sustainability. Gina La Morte, founder of socially conscious label, Trade by Gina La Morte, says that "conscious fashion is everything from the production to the paper goods to the supply chain. Everything about a company should strive to be sustainable in every aspect."[8]

The future of the industry lies in building a type of business that not only promotes sustainable production but can grow and help people work. Trade by Gina La Morte is a holistically sustainable brand that supports single mothers and human trafficking victims through its ethical business model.[8]

The Slow Factory is a fashion tech lab producing accessories and apparel with high-resolution NASA images on Italian silks.[9] Each unique collection promotes a message of activism and environmental awareness. It's exciting to see so many brands embrace sustainability in all aspects of the business.

* * *

According to an article in *The Business of Fashion*, millennials' interest in sustainable fashion fails to align with the reality of their purchasing patterns.[10] In 2017 alone, millennials spent two hundred billion dollars, and it is estimated that by the end of 2018, millennials will have exceeded this amount to have more spending power than any prior generation.[10] Clearly millennials have a distinct set of values and preferences, which seems to include an interest in sustainable fashion.

Millennials care a lot about sustainable fashion, even willingly choosing to switch loyalty from brands that don't promote sustainable production to more ethical options. But what are they actually buying from these brands? Another study by Oeko-Tex revealed that only 34 percent of millennials admit to buying from sustainable brands.[11] Part of the problem could be that there is not enough product availability and effective marketing to cater toward this demographic's needs.

It seems that millennials struggle to find sustainable brands that meet their expectations on quality and price point. And when it comes down to it, other factors like uniqueness of product, accessibility, and affordability trump sustainability. While millennial consumers state an interest in sustainable brands, the reality is that few labels promote ethical production. A few are:

- Patagonia

- Everlane
- Reformation

The next few chapters explore ethical production in fashion as well as the movers and shakers at the forefront of this movement.

Natalie Massenet

Natalie Massenet, the serial fashion-preneur who founded luxury ecommerce site, Net-a-Porter, launched a venture capital firm focusing on the intersection of technology and retail in direct-to-consumer fashion startups.[12] In an interview with *The Business of Fashion*, Natalie acknowledges that consumers desire newness above all.[13] It could just be that the brands best able to balance newness with affordability and sustainability will experience the most success.[13]

Social media makes it easier than ever to discover new brands. With this heightened visibility, though, brands must never lose sight of who their customer is and what he or she wants. "The businesses that will endure will be those that build their strategies around an authentic understanding of their consumers and never lose sight of them as they grow," Massenet says.[13] I think the most successful fashion companies will learn to balance all their consumers' desires, including sustainability.

* * *

So if millennials truly care about sustainability, but feel it falls secondary to other factors like newness and affordability, how can companies effectively engage with these young consumers to get them to prioritize caring for ethical fashion? And do companies even care? With the rise of fast fashion brands like H&M or Forever 21, the industry is shifting toward a means of production that looks after big business interest.

Sustainability is just a piece of the puzzle, and it won't even matter unless brands also meet consumers' price point while demonstrating product uniqueness. For consumers to care, brands must take an all-in approach.

Another problem is that the sustainability information for these brands is not always easily accessible for consumers. Instead of lengthy reports hidden in a brand's website, the focus should be on making sustainability information quick, easy, and digestible. Millennials claim to value sustainable clothing, so brands must emphasize and effectively market ethical production to appeal to this consumer base. It will be key to strike a balance between all the factors that consumers consider.

But getting consumers to care about ethical fashion when there are so many quicker and cheaper options unsurprisingly proves to be difficult. Fast fashion is just so, well, *easy.* A 2016 report by McKinsey revealed that nearly three-fifths of all clothing ends up in incinerators or landfills within a year of being made.[14] So although today's consumers value sustainability, the reality is that most clothing is not made to last and ends up in the garbage.

Reformation

But what about the fashion brands that *do* promote ethical production? Although few and far between, there are in fact some companies committed to the ethics of slow fashion. Reformation's online shopping tool, RefScale, shows consumers how much waste they will contribute in buying a Reformation product versus a less-sustainable option like a cotton t-shirt.[15]

"A typical cotton t-shirt uses two hundred gallons of water," claims former-model-turned-CEO Yael Aflalo.[15]

Yael's efforts to boost sustainable fashion are certainly having an impact. Her Tencel tee collection in particular sparked interest in the sustainability movement with its graphic tees featuring catchy phrases like "Do it for Leo" and "F*ck Cotton."[15]

And the whole collection only uses six gallons of water to produce.[15] Compared to its wasteful counterpart, a cotton t-shirt, I'd say Reformation is spot on with finding ecological solutions to marry sustainability with style.

"It's the perfect example of where the industry should be moving. Reformation is for a new generation of customers who want to consume with purpose," says Russian fashion entrepreneur Miroslava Duma.[16]

* * *

Purposeful fashion consumption speaks to a broader cultural trend in sharing. From the increased prevalence of ride-share apps like Uber and Lyft to subscription-based entertainment services like Netflix and Spotify, the landscape is shifting to support on-demand services that replace ownership.

For Days, the latest sustainable fashion venture by serial entrepreneur Kristy Caylor, uses an on-demand business model to encourage customers to upcycle old clothes.[17] Consumers pay anywhere between $12 and $36 a month for access to recycled cotton t-shirts, which they can return or exchange at any time.[17]

With millennial consumption expected to rise to 45 percent of the global luxury goods market by 2025, our days of ownership may be over.[17] "I think a huge portion of what we wear in the future is going to be comprised of things we don't own forever," says founder and chief executive Jennifer Hyman, of Rent the Runway.[18]

Companies are starting to learn that their customers value having more options through renting over ownership. Hyman claims that consumers would rather have limited access to designer goods for the price of one article of clothing at Zara. And if brands can do so in an ethical and circular fashion, that helps, too.

Consuming sustainably and with purpose is fashion's new frontier.

Elizabeth St. John

Eco-friendly designer, Elizabeth St. John, of Elizabeth St. John Couture, prides herself on running a thoughtful fashion brand.

Elizabeth St. John Couture is a bridal wear atelier specializing in sustainable, hand-crafted, customized gowns. Liz told me that she originally started her company with the goal of reducing waste in production.[19] In fashion, creating one-of-a-kind gowns typically results in much wasted fabric. Liz sought new ways to reduce waste in production by incorporating traditionally wasted fabric back into the garment, be it through additional accents or accessories.

Bridal wear is already super expensive, so Liz welcomed any way to save a bit in the process. Sometimes the leftover fabric would be included as additional stitching for the same gown, and other times it would be added to a different one. Liz makes accessories, hand-made flowers, and details for other gowns with her extra material.

"So much now is driven by price that it will be difficult to be 100 percent sustainable," Liz tells me. "I migrated to more sustainable fibers, which are typically not natural fibers (like polyester made of recycled bottles)."[19]

The natural fibers that are sustainable, like cotton, require tons of water. Organic cotton requires double the amount. And Liz always searches for ways to be sustainable in production. Elizabeth St. John does not print catalogs and runs her atelier entirely on wind power. This is all in an effort to cut back on waste and still give the customer what she wants.[19]

And to make bridal wear, Liz tells me that she works in reverse. Whereas traditional bridal fashion houses create sketches and then source materials based off of the sketches, Liz finds her materials first. She tells me that she looks for what inspires her and finds a way to incorporate it into a bridal gown.[19]

"I design based off of the materials I find," Liz says.[19] "So I'm inspired by the material rather than having to source it based on my sketches."

Because she works in reverse, Liz finds she is better able to help customers create a dream gown rather than force them to choose based off of existing creations. "I can work with you with what you envision and what I can source," she shares.[19] This business model gives Liz the liberty to create custom, sustainable gowns based on her customers' specific preferences. Right now, Liz tells me she is very inspired by lightweight wool, as the material gives her really interesting results when she manipulates it.

Whether creating a gown with frayed edges to resemble feathers or sourcing the latest nylons and silks from England, Elizabeth St. John is making her impact and normalizing sustainable fashion with her gorgeous creations.

POWER OF CELEBRITIES IN SUSTAINABILITY

In 2017, sisters Kim Kardashian and Kylie Jenner both were celebrated for their "sustainable fashion choices" of wearing plastic dresses.[20]

One problem, said some experts. The process of making PVC (the plastic in their dresses) actually creates some of the most toxic substances.[21]

* * *

Celebrities carry a particular cultural capital that allows them to influence and have an impact on followers' consumer choices. Oftentimes, the message that celebrities endorse through their advertising campaigns carries weight in broadening social cultural acceptance. Yet there's a difference between what celebrities say about sustainable clothing and their actual buying habits. Celebrity activists use their influence to promote their vision of a better life, yet at times it appears they are merely projecting.

In today's age of influencers, celebrities and social media influencers wield all the power in communicating directly to consumers. And nowadays, anyone with a phone can become a global influencer. But what does it take to capture the attention of today's young consumer?

Textile dyeing is the second largest polluter after agriculture. Many celebrities have taken a stand on the issues of excess waste and environmental degradation associated with fast fashion in particular. The obsession with immediate access to fashion promotes a throwaway culture, shortening the lifespan of clothing. The Rana Plaza disaster in Bangladesh in 2013, where more than one thousand garment workers died in a clothing factory's collapse, raised awareness on the dangers of fast fashion.[22] These concerns were amplified by the voices of celebrities who engaged in the promotion of ethically produced clothing.

* * *

Stella McCartney, for instance, has been an avid supporter of sustainable fashion throughout her career. Her focus on environmental production and eco-friendly materials opens up the conversation around conscious fashion.[21]

Many other celebrities, including Emma Watson, have joined the sustainable fashion conversation. Watson has served as the Women Goodwill Ambassador since 2010 and actively advocates for environmental causes and women's rights. I think we need more people like her and Gina to put a holistic approach to sustainability on the public's radar.

Threats of Fast Fashion on the Circular Economy

Many fashion brands have committed themselves to circularity across the supply chain. But are these brands actually less wasteful?

Circularity in the fashion industry refers to the reuse of materials, discouraging the typical production and waste cycle of clothing. According to a 2017 study by the Ellen MacArthur Foundation, fifty-three million tons of clothing are produced globally each year, of which 87 percent is ultimately either incinerated or dumped in landfills.[24]

At the 2017 Copenhagen Fashion Summit, fashion brands made a commitment to employ a completely circular fashion system by 2020.[23] Together, all of the brands that push for a more sustainable fashion cycle account for 12 percent of the global apparel market, according to the Global Fashion Agenda.[25]

The only way we're going to get there is to change business models," said Annie Gullingsrud, who works with brands such as Eileen Fisher, H&M, and Stella McCartney at the Cradle to Cradle Products Innovation Institute, a nonprofit working toward increased sustainable manufacturing.[26] "That means keeping materials in circulation for as long as possible, thus cutting down on the use of virgin materials."

But even though most clothing goes to waste, it is important to remember that progress has been made already toward holistic sustainability. Many brands embrace the ethical fashion movement and incorporate circularity into their business models.

For example, Inditex, the biggest fashion group in the world that owns brands like Zara and Massimo Dutti, works with nonprofit Caritas to install garment collection bins in major cosmopolitan centers.[27] Inditex pledged to invest 1.5 million dollars toward garment collection and recycling improvements.[27] H&M was one of the first brands in 2012 to institute a global clothing collection initiative, and since 2015, H&M has offered grants to companies and startups with the most innovative ideas in closed-loop textiles.[27]

Americans dispose of around twenty-six billion pounds of clothing each year.[28] Embracing circularity across the whole fashion value chain means incorporating new design technologies to combat the wastefulness of fast fashion. The problem of overconsumption in clothing has grown to be massive and must be tackled, and soon. From a business perspective, it is not to a brand's advantage to promote the throwaway culture, as it just encourages an attitude of overconsumption.

The idea is that consumers should be investing only in clothing with long-term value to them. Brands today must find ways to give consumers easy options to dispose of unwanted garments and encourage meaningful purchases. Discouraging a fast fashion cycle that promotes throwaway culture will emphasize to consumers the shift in values toward sustainability.

Sustainability as Explosive Growth Strategy

Instagram is a powerful tool for casting agencies and millennial consumers alike to acquire information on the latest trends. You can travel the whole world in five minutes, and that is the new competitive edge. But fashion is historically slow to make change, and who knows how long it will take before we fully reap the benefits of social-media-promoted sustainable fashion.

We are on the brink of something huge that will completely alter our understanding of fashion and how we shop with sustainability in mind. Companies like Gucci and Versace have already stated they will no longer make fur.[29] With all of the technological advancements in our world, there is no reason why we should continue to endanger animals when we have the capabilities of producing stylish, faux products that will end up looking the same, if not better, than the real thing.

Laura Lee, of Laura Lee Designs, says that people crave diversity to show their uniqueness.[30] Consumers today love luxury products but care about sustainable development. Gucci has made headlines for their explosive growth strategy, which is rooted in sustainability and brand experience. In fact, the statistics show that 50 percent of customers purchasing luxury products from brands like Gucci are millennials.[31]

Interesting that these consumers choose to spend their disposable income on luxury. Whereas before, luxury was geared toward appealing to middle to older aged women, now luxury brands are going to have to make a shift to find ways to engage with millennials, their new main customers.

And this is where data comes in to play. What things do millennials care about and consider important? It is clear that sites like Pinterest Tumblr, and Instagram are hugely influential for consumers who want to discover the next big thing. I believe that brand focus on sustainability across the supply chain will prove to be a main driver of growth in the coming years.

What to Watch for:

- Consumer shift in focus to supporting sustainable fashion
- More brands aligning themselves with values supporting a holistic approach to sustainability
- I believe that in the next twenty years, we will see a movement of brands toward embracing ethical production and seeking different ways to capture the attention of millennials. Be it through social media, escalated e-commerce efforts, or an elevated retail experience in physical stores, brands are picking up on the fact that they need to embrace the sustainability movement to survive.
- Millennials also value ease of use for products, so the ability to filter products by terms such as fair trade or organic will certainly sway consumers.
- Celebrities who not only promote a sustainable message in fashion but also practice this behavior themselves will find their message resonates more with consumers.
- Consumers shift away from fast fashion and toward investment in clothing with long-term wear.

PART 2

TECHNOLOGY

44 hits. Not too shabby. I'm standing at the Dynavision board in the OT gym during an afternoon of cognitive therapy (more like cognitive hell) and record my score. It's already an improvement, considering I only managed to hit 31 buttons in a single trial a few months earlier.

* * *

Not only did I become paralyzed on my left side from suffering a stroke, but I also lost half of my peripheral field of vision and for awhile suffered mild spatial neglect. The spatial, or in my case, left-side neglect, meant my brain didn't see things on my left side. It's so weird—I've been known to walk into signs right in front of me, because I didn't see them there.

I used the Dynavision board at therapy to help address my visual neglect issues. Staring at the board and tapping the buttons that light up, while boring and tedious, teaches my brain to pay attention to images on my left side. My neglect is virtually gone now, thanks to the practice with vision technology, but I still find it difficult and frustrating at times to remember to scan across the entirety of whatever is in front of me to ensure that I see it all.

Things as simple as seeing all the food on my plate were challenges in the beginning. My mom started to place my dessert on the left side of my plate because she knew that I would be sure to scan to find it. I went to the movies for the first time over Thanksgiving, and I quickly learned that I couldn't see the entire movie screen without physically turning my head so the picture was right in my central field of vision.

With a lot of hard work and awesome vision therapy technology, I've come a tremendous way. The majority of my neglect issues have resolved, but I still have to make an active effort with my visual attention. I continue to improve, getting one step closer to leading an independent and functional life.

AI Chatbots and the Rise of the See-Now-Buy-Now Model

Whether we like it or not, artificial intelligence already incorporates itself into fashion. The industry itself is on the verge of a major technological disruption as we continue to see advancements in improving the retail experience. Global revenue from artificial intelligence is expected to grow rapidly from $643.7 million in 2016 to $36.8 billion by 2025.[32]

You may not realize it, but even today, you interact with artificial intelligence regularly. Many brands rely on chatbots to drive sales and make customized recommendations to their target consumers. And chatbots do more than just recommend products.[33] They can help consumers identify and act on their preferences.

* * *

I have been on the hunt for a cute romper to wear in the summer for a few months now but have failed to find the perfect one. Not only would it have to fit my body, it also needs a front clasp. Because my left fingers can't yet reach around to my back and maneuver a clasp, I need a garment option that either does not have buttons or has clasps in the front where I can manage with one hand.

I logged onto the H&M website (after all, I am still living like a college student on a budget) and began my search. On the site, I started a chat with agent Ana, who helped me find a romper I could wear that didn't involve any difficult buttons or clasps. In this instance, interacting with a chatbot proved to be super helpful because it managed to search through the clothing items and make recommendations quicker than I would have been able to do it on my own. Ana listened to my requests and preferences and then made informed recommendations for me. Chatbots and virtual assistants are used by many brands to respond to customer inquiries about specific products, and their capabilities will only further develop.

Some older fashion houses like Burberry employ chatbots over messenger to reveal a behind-the-scenes look at the latest collections.[34] With the see-now-buy-now model, the six-month delay of runway looks to the store disappears. Consumers are welcome to purchase looks they see immediately. Burberry followed in the footsteps of Tommy Hilfiger, launching a chatbot to focus on this see-now-buy-now model, which caters to consumers' desire for instant gratification.

Burberry differentiates its fashion bot from those of other brands as an outlet offering unique and authentic footage of the operations of a major fashion house.[3] After scrolling through pages of designs and inspirational blurbs, viewers are prompted to purchase the clothing they viewed.

Neda Whitney, group account director for R/GA, spoke to *Glossy* in an interview about linking bots to fashion week collections. The potential for fashion bots "brings up a new avenue for communication. It's going to drive a lot of awareness," she said.[34] "Bots are still such a new space that we will have to see how customers react and grow with it, but there's a lot of room for brands to start that."

High-end fashion brands are moving toward the see-now-buy-now model as it speeds up the fashion cycle, allowing consumers to purchase clothing immediately after viewing it on the runway for the first time.[34] No more waiting six months for the latest trends to hit the shelves.

Although many fashion houses have begun to put out collections more frequently than twice a year, the vast majority of brands have been slow to adopt the see-now-buy-now model. The timing of product releases has become difficult to coordinate as companies struggle to balance the demand for new products with their long production cycles and slow turnaround for public release. Even though more brands are adopting the see-now-buy-now model, the practice is far from becoming industry-standard.

Chief Executive of Mulberry, Thierry Andretta, spoke in an interview with *The Business of Fashion* about shifting consumer standards to favor immediate gratification. "As soon as [the customer] found something online, they want to buy it immediately. If it's not there, in the majority of the cases ... they will not wait for months," Andretta states.[35]

This example highlights an interesting trend in consumer behavior. Consumers, especially millennials, desire the ease of immediate purchase, instead of waiting months until runway looks hit the stores.

* * *

The traditional fashion cycle consists of seasonally presented collections twice a year in major fashion hubs like Paris, Milan, London, and New York. The Spring/Summer season shows in September, and the fall/winter season in February. Collection items typically do not appear in stores until six months to a year later.

The industry is beginning to acknowledge the potential benefits of switching to a business model that favors consumers' desire for instant gratification. The conventional cycle is not enough to capture and retain the attention and loyalty of consumers. The see-now-buy-now model completely alters consumers' expectations for fashion consumption, allowing them to instantly purchase the runway looks shown.

Consumers can view runway looks and then buy them in real time. The increasing globalization and digitalization of our world contributes to the growing irrelevance of what used to be a strict showing season calendar. Consumers are starting to ask more frequently: why buy into one-season trends when instead I could invest in a piece that will last me years?

To a generation that grew up in a digital world powered by social media, instant gratification has become a standard expectation. Instagram direct message, Facebook, and Twitter serve as effective platforms for consumers to grab a company's attention and express their concerns and vice versa. In order to survive in the constantly evolving world of fashion, the transition to a brand culture fueled by instant gratification will be necessary.

Because social media has become such a powerful tool for brand promotion, influencers are on the rise, lauded for wielding immense power in brand promotion. Celebrities like Kim Kardashian West and Selena Gomez get paid hundreds of thousands of dollars per sponsored Instagram post to endorse a specific brand or product.[36]

Although fashion is experiencing an expanding influencer market, the challenge of determining the quality of the account's followers and the rate of their engagement with sponsored posts still exists. Since the landscape is still so new, the opportunity has arisen for many third-party services to connect brands with social media influencers, who oftentimes buy fake followers to boost their following.[36]

Instead of contracting with influencers for their following, brands should focus on paying the influencers based on actual engagement with their posts to avoid falling into the fake follower trap. And here data analytics come into play. "A brand that's not prepared to invest time and money to study the space is setting itself up for failure," writes Amy Odell in *The Business of Fashion*.[37] By studying the space and doing the proper research on the success metrics of influencers, brands can get a better idea of the proper compensation and how well the influencers will be able to achieve their goals for brand interaction.

Amazon Prime caters toward the consumer desire for instant gratification by eliminating long wait times to receive packages. Voice activated personal assistants like Alexa and Siri cut down on processing time by eliminating the need to type inquiries.[38]

And fortunately, with advancements in technology, instant gratification is becoming more achievable for fashion brands. In fact, the ability to immediately purchase already tampers with the traditional trend cycle.

Apart from artificially intelligent chatbots, technology is being utilized to further transform the fashion landscape. Google has already begun testing the effectiveness of artificially intelligent fashion designers.[39] Could the future of AI render human fashion designers irrelevant? I'm not sure, but I do know that many companies are working on advancing the capabilities of artificial intelligence to deal with consumer inquiries.

Google tested the powers of artificial intelligence for fashion with Project Muze and the German fashion platform Zalando.[39] Using neural networks, Project Muze's artificial intelligence generated algorithms to create designs based off users' style preferences.[39]

Amazon has also hopped on board, using machine learning to assess whether or not an article of clothing is considered stylish. Amazon patented a manufacturing system to create apparel en masse.[38] Think of it like fast fashion by Amazon.

But it will still be awhile before brands make the complete switchover to human-free design. While AI has incredible capabilities in shaping and adapting to consumer preferences, there is still a long way to go before human designers are rendered irrelevant.

AI already provides assistance in the creation of designs, but the problem is that these sketches are not always runway-ready. I believe in the coming years we will continue to see Artificial Intelligence create and iterate on designs with increased accuracy. Today, human designers can access information from Artificial Intelligence systems to predict and influence fashion trends. Human designers rely on the algorithms of artificial intelligence to help shape future collections.

Advancements in Wearable Tech

"*Whoever thought that walking could be so challenging?*" I ask myself as I struggle to maneuver my legs, which are enclosed in a robot Eksoskeleton. "Weight shift forward more. You're leaning back," says the physical therapist accompanying me on my walk. *Weird,* I think, as I try to extend my left hip and flex at the knee. *Am I not already shifted forward?*

On top of my biweekly physical and occupational therapy, I participated in a four-week research study that assesses the walking gait of stroke patients in an eksoskeleton. Once in the robot, I walk around for thirty minutes. It takes all the concentration ability I possess to internalize how it feels for my leg to walk in a correct pattern. The robot helps normalize my walking, so I walk perfectly, albeit slowly. I struggle to remember how the leg movement and foot placement feels so I can recreate the pattern outside of the robot in my daily life.

It's pretty cool to me, as a traumatic brain injury patient who limps and can't effectively isolate each component of a deceivingly complex task like walking, that I can strap myself into a robot that helps me walk correctly and eliminates the irregular patterns I've developed as a form of compensation. I never appreciated before how complex the act of walking is, but now it seems that thinking about it is all I do. *Heel strike, watch your foot placement, stabilize the ankle, bend at the knee, extend at the hip. Over and over again. Constantly thinking and reminding myself of these actions every time I take a step.* I realized if I don't focus on these motions that I once took for granted, my body won't execute them.

And when I really think about it, it's also pretty cool to me that the technology to normalize walking exists. According to an article in *Forbes*, the wearable tech market is expected to double by 2021.[40] In the next few years, we can expect to see an increase in the number of wearable devices produced at more affordable prices. Software developers continue to improve the experience of wearable technology, finding new ways to ensure that the hardware provides insightful data to the user. The International Data Corporation estimates that by 2021, the wearable tech market will have undergone a compound annual growth rate of 76.1 percent.[41]

We already experience the future implications of wearable technology in our lives. From Apple watches and Fitbits to Beats headphones, wearable technology and the Internet of Things will only continue to improve the quality of our lives. It is wild to think that one day, probably very soon, someone like me wouldn't need to walk in an Eksoskeleton robot to improve her gait because the technology will just be infused into her jeans or sneakers. And that day literally can't come soon enough.

3-D printing

The idea of mass customization and 3D printing was first utilized in the medical field, but it has since expanded to encompass other industries, including fashion. Kristen Plate, author of *Printed to the Nines: Why 3D Printing Will Transform the Fashion Industry*, explains the 3-D printing process and shows readers the implications of the additive manufacturing process for revolutionizing the fashion industry.[42]

3-D printing is beginning to infiltrate more and more aspects of fashion. Kristen references the first 3D printed bikini, N12, as an example of the potential for innovation and creativity in the space.[42] 3-D printing affords designers the chance to get creative in accommodating for groups of people that otherwise would have no way to access the fashion industry.

In her book, Kristen mentions Stephen Nigro, head of 3D printing at HP. He wonders if it is possible that we will use 3D printing in the future for clothing, and what would need to occur in order for this practice to become commonplace.[42] Nigro believes 3D printing will help us produce faster but not necessarily contribute to a thriving consumer market.[36] In today's world, there still remain lots of barriers to entry in 3-D printed fashion.

For example, 3-D printing has the potential to solve the issue of two different sized feet. How cool would it be to just print out two shoes custom fit to your feet? I currently struggle with the issue of finding footwear to accommodate my physical limitations. Due to my injury, I need to wear a leg brace that helps me lift my foot to walk. I hate it, and can't wait for the day when my ankle is strong enough to walk without a brace. But until that day, I resign myself to wearing a toe-off leg brace every time I leave the house.

My brain injury has left me with dropfoot, a condition caused by paralysis of the anterior muscles in the leg, restricting normal gait patterns. With drop foot, I am unable to lift my toes to walk with ease. Instead, when I pick up my left leg it flops down unceremoniously and completely flat-footed.

One of the biggest problems I face in dealing with drop foot is finding appropriate footwear that can accommodate my brace. I can't tell you how many times I have gone to the store and tried on a shoe that I thought would work with my brace, only to realize that something about it doesn't fit right. It is extremely difficult to find somewhat fashionable shoes to wear with my brace.

And heels? *Out of the question.* My options are basically limited to traditional, closed-toe tennis shoes. Not fun for a girl who loves honing her style and spends her free time browsing runway looks and reading fashion blogs.

This got me thinking. Why do fashion houses refuse to design for the needs of customers with physical limitations? Granted, I'd never even really thought about a more accessible fashion myself until its nonexistence directly applied to me, but I know there is absolutely no reason why fashion cannot be both adaptive and beautiful.

I hope in the future 3-D clothing will become more commonplace. How cool would it be if one day I could use 3D printing to create a pair of cute custom shoes that I'm able to wear? I miss the option of wearing shoes that aren't tennis shoes. And for the most part, I can't even wear trendy sneakers because the heel isn't lifted up enough. How crazy would it be if I could print a pair of stylish trainers or wedged heels that were custom fit to my foot and worked with my brace?

Biofabricated Leathers

The implications for biofabrication in fashion are huge.

* * *

Modern Meadow is transforming the ways in which we use biofabricated materials to make everyday goods. "The history of humanity can be tracked with our development of materials. At first, humans took from nature and mastered materials like wool, leather and cotton. In the seventies we mastered polymers and created synthetic materials with performance properties better than natural fibers, like nylon, polyester and Kevlar. Today, biofabrication allows us to take the best of natural materials and combine it with the performance of synthetics to be more sustainable than ever. Bringing together nature's toolbox and human ingenuity—it's a very exciting time in material innovation," shares the Modern Meadow team.[43]

The design team decided to reinterpret the graphic tee using biofabricated materials, provoking new ideas on the implications of biofabrication in leather. Modern Meadow's creation of the first bioleather materials brand, Zoa, leaves a minimal carbon footprint and combines seamlessly with other materials.[44] Zoa provokes new ideas on the implications of these animal-friendly materials in leather.[44]

What to Watch for:

- The diminishment of the trend cycle to accommodate customer desire for instant gratification
- More brands begin to embrace the see-now-buy now model
- Improvements in artificial intelligence will increase the role machines play in the fashion design and production process.
- Artificial Intelligence will further hone skills to design and generate customized recommendations based off of a customer's style preferences.

- Anticipate that as technology continues to improve, we will see more and more cool technology incorporated into garments.
- 3-D printing expanding beyond the medical field to fashion with the creation of the first 3-D printed bikini.
- 3-D printed fashion is still in its early stages, but designers will continue to push the boundaries of the industry to show us what is possible with manipulation of textiles.
- More animal-friendly materials will be used in leather to accommodate socially conscious consumers.

PART 3

SOLIDARITY FOR A CAUSE—AUTHENTIC BRAND MESSAGING

"That's what is so fun about fashion: You have the ability to kind of reinvent yourself every day."

—ULLA JOHNSON

Consumers increasingly want to support brands that foster a sense of community as well as share a positive message. While this idea may not seem novel, the difference today is that brands realize now it is essential for them to engage directly with their customers and support the same values if they want to survive.

Brands expressing solidarity with popular causes like LGBTQ or women's rights are becoming more commonplace. For example, Nike has supported the LGBTQ community with its annual BETRUE pride campaign since 2012.[45] A 2017 survey from Omnicom Group emphasized that 70 percent of millennials would be willing to spend more money on brands they genuinely care about.[46] So for fashion brands, this means it is essential to align your company with consumer values. Today's consumer wants more than just a product. She wants to buy from brands that actually stand for a message.

And consumers are ready to pounce and attack even the slightest error fashion companies make. For this reason I believe many brands shy away from aligning with consumer values and taking a political stance. They fear offending and igniting the ire of consumers. It's a fine line companies walk.

* * *

In 2017, a Kendall Jenner ad sparked intense controversy because of its dismissal of the Black Lives Matter movement.[47] Cody Chandler, who has worked on ad campaigns for the likes of Adidas, Versace, and Stella McCartney, understands that fashion brands tread on thin ice. "Everyone wants to act like they are socially conscious, but they know the [consequences] of one mistake," he says.[48] Our society is so quick to judge that oftentimes messages can get misconstrued.

Brands may be afraid to take an even remotely political stance because of the consequences for offending potential consumers. However, I believe this is even more reason for brands to remain steadfast in their beliefs and align their company with consumer values. Backing a specific set of values and sharing a positive message does not isolate customers; it draws them in.

Political Engagement and Value System Alignment

Consumers of younger generatins like millennials and Gen Z expect brands to take a stance and support political causes.

The key is finding ways to show companies that they can engage with sustainable movements and still be profitable. While there is a movement of young people toward increased sustainability in fashion, the challenge of getting the supply chain to catch up with today's speed of communication still exists.

Gucci donated $500,000 to the young people leading the 2018 March for Our Lives. In *The Business of Fashion Inside Fashion* podcast, Gucci Chief Marco Bizzarri stated, "We don't take stands if there is no relation to what we do."[49] A Gucci employee was killed in the Orlando shooting, and so the brand decided to donate this money to the March, believing that the gesture effectively supports a cause in a very real and quick way.[49]

The March for Our Lives supports the kind of values Gucci wants to instill in their employees and in their company. While fashion companies typically tend to shy away from taking a political stance, Bizzarri believes getting behind this march quickly shows that the brand is committed to its cause.

"We were as a company affected and very impressed by the capability of young people to express themselves," Bizzarri tells *The Business of Fashion.*[49]

Furthermore, Bizzarri believes that corporate neutrality is completely finished. "You need as a company to take a stand because in most of the cases governments are not taking stands," Bizzarri says.[49] "We were emotionally linked to the march," he continues. "It represents the types of values in protest and standing up for your beliefs that Gucci wishes to instill in their company culture."

I believe we will continue to see brands integrating their system of values and beliefs with those of consumers. Gucci has set a great example and might actually be one of the few exceptions to the standard luxury consumer, who tends to be older, wealthier, and uninterested in mixing politics with commerce. But times are changing. As millennials rise to have the most purchasing power of any generation, they vocalize their desire for brand community and value systems. J.D. Ostrow, chief marketing officer of Theory, believes that the days of influential consumers neglecting brand value alignment are numbered. He says brands that abstain from political conversations risk alienating consumers. "Not being involved isn't an option," he said in an email statement.[50] "[Young people] are drawn to it because that's what change demands and what the new cultural consciousness is creating."

Fashion to Address Social Problems

The importance of branding to portray a set of values consumers can support has never been more relevant. This brand-value alignment movement is causing a major cultural moment, rooted in the past. Robin Givhan, fashion editor for *The Washington Post*, wrote about how fashion influenced the personal branding of activists in the Civil Rights Movement. The sixties were characterized by suits, slim-fitting ties, and whiteness. While stuck in this stagnant, traditional and backward-looking culture, Givhan says that "the fashion industry did its part to try to move the culture forward with the sexual freedom implied by miniskirts."[51]

But even back then, change was slow. As our country teetered on the brink of collapse with the Vietnam War and persistent cultural and racial inequalities, fashion gravitated toward maintenance of the mainstream idealist attitude. Ignorance of social problems became the new manifesto. By refusing to acknowledge these issues we negated their existence.

In this era of cultural and societal misgivings, fashion became a tool for self-expression used to demonstrate political identities. And so fashion spurred a cultural upheaval. It didn't take much to make a statement with style, considering the white establishment defined itself with conventional fashion. The flowing peasant skirts the hippies flashed contrasted drastically with white middle-class style.[51]

Givhan elaborates on hippie style in the sixties as a tool to share and broadcast a specific message: "Their style reflected their ideology and their aspirations. Their clothes were costumes that they slipped on; they were integral to their story. The hippies were method actors, living deep inside their performance. They set out to aggravate and irritate. They were indecorous. They were turning on to drugs and tuning out; but they could always tune back in, and society would welcome them back."[51]

And today especially, we see fashion utilized as a tool to confront the prominent social issues plaguing our society. Kerby Jean-Raymond, designer of luxury label Pyer Moss, seeks to construct a narrative of heritage and political activism through his clothing. The Pyer Moss Fall 2018 line, "American Also," explores the origins of the term "cowboy," a word originally used to describe black laborers in a derogatory way, but has since become whitewashed.[52]

Raymond effectively employs fashion to tackle social issues. For his Fall 2015 show, the Brooklyn designer screened a fifteen-minute video on police brutality and the black community.[52] He received death threats from the KKK for this choice, but that didn't stop him.

Robin Givhan tells me that the power of fashion lies in its ability to comment on current culture.[53] "A narrative tells you something about the way the clothes connect to the culture in this moment," she shares. "It's not just about the design, it's also about the message that is conveyed by that brand."[53]

For Fall 2018, Raymond chose music as his medium to convey a message of black empowerment.[52] With the assistance of singer-songwriter Raphael Saadiq, Raymond shared his message of black empowerment through uplifting gospel choirs.[52] Although the music definitely inspired, I think the most uplifting message of all was the statement of empowerment to see a young black designer leading his own fashion house and paving the way for future creatives, redefining the realm of possibility.

Politics and Fashion

From JFK to Hillary Clinton, fashion has played a critical role in politics. For decades, politicians have tapped into the power of fashion to assist in promoting their ideas. Fashion, in fact, was a key component of the Nazi ideology. Just take a look at the Hitler mustache and how it has remained taboo for half a century. Clean-cut faces and tailored uniforms exude an image of power and organization.

Fashion has the power to convey a curated message, and this power can easily be abused by the wrong groups. Alt-right movements across the country have shown Americans that white supremacists can ditch the traditional white cloak and hood in favor of a new uniform. White supremacists today resemble your average Joe, clad in a polo shirt and khaki pants.

What prompted this style change? White supremacists attempted to co-opt the sneaker brand New Balance as "the official shoes of white people."[54] Neo-Nazi leaders know they need to fully embrace fashion and update their personal style to better get their message across and appeal to Americans.

Richard Spencer, founder of the hate site *The Daily Stormer* and vocal white supremacist, articulated the importance of appearance at white supremacist rallies. "We need to be extremely conscious of what we look like and how we present ourselves. That matters more than our ideas. If that is sad to you, I'm sorry, but that is just human nature."[55]

In the past, Neo-Nazi groups and white supremacists have existed on the fringes of society, and their style choices emphasized this divide. However, now white supremacists are turning toward the everyday conservative American look of khakis and button-downs to normalize their core tenets and beliefs. They understand the importance of image in projecting a message. The rebranding of white supremacists as clean-cut, khaki-wearing everyday people has succeeded in portraying them as relatable. It is incredibly frightening to me that Neo-Nazis are adapting into mainstream culture and using style as a weapon in promoting their hate-filled ideology.[56]

In December 2017, the hipster-Marxist magazine *Jacobin* published an online essay, "The Elite Roots of Richard Spencer's Racism," that sought to understand the leader's white supremacist views. "He represents a common and longstanding (if overlooked) phenomenon: the well-educated and financially comfortable bigot," the author, Michael Phillips, wrote.[55] "His blend of racism and elitism represents only an extreme version of a worldview that has long prevailed among the affluent in Spencer's hometown."[55]

If something as simple as New Balance sneakers and khaki pants are able to be co-opted in support of hateful causes, how do we know if we can trust the ideology behind this fashion shift? With the changing nature of protest fashion and activism in general, it can be hard to discern between true authentic messaging from brands that actually stand behind the causes they claim to support, and brands and groups that take advantage of and exploit cultural norms to support their own racist agenda. Fred Perry polos and khaki pants are a prime example of a co-option of traditionally conservative apparel to promote a radically different political agenda.

I believe it is important to think about what we want the brands and products we purchase to say about us and consider the messaging that the support of these brands conveys. Are we just buying into the latest trend, or do we actually support the message of the brand and its products?

We live in a time where politics and fashion are increasingly intertwined, and clearly this connection extends to hateful causes of white supremacism as well.

Givhan has written on fashion's failure to comment on the racial hatred invoked at the nationalist march in Charlottesville, North Carolina. "Many fashion brands have built their businesses on the mythic melting pot of the American Dream. Fashion owes an especially large debt to those communities targeted by white supremacists: Designers regularly draw artistic inspiration from communities of color," Givhan writes.[50] If fashion draws such extensive inspiration from these underrepresented communities, wouldn't it make sense to think that the industry would do whatever it can to stick up for these communities, even at the very least for the purpose of preserving the business?

Fashion today reaches a much wider audience. Givhan writes that it has transformed into "a stealth weapon" for white supremacists who have totally bought into "fashion's ability to camouflage, distract, embolden, reassure, flatter and, quite simply, lie. White nationalists are moving through communities cloaked in the most mundane, banal kind of fashion—clothes that do not inspire a double-take. Clothes that are acceptable and appropriate. Clothes that make them look like they belong. And the fashion industry has yet to tell them that they do not."[56]

Neo-Nazis are turning to fashion as a means of self-expression, and they are doing so in the normal clothes of everyday people. No white cloaks and hoods are involved. Everyday dress almost makes white supremacists look relatable. When will fashion learn that we need to shut it down? Denouncing white nationalism would show people that the fashion industry is not allowing this hatred to be normalized.

* * *

Fashion is a medium that speaks cross-culturally and can be leveraged in support of various causes. While fashion can promote hateful, racist messages, it can also spread a message of activism in our contentious political climate. This is all wonderful, but it does raise the question of intention. Do we actually care about women's rights and decide to actively address this issue, or are we just buying into the latest trends? This is the question we have to consider, realizing that whether we like it or not, the clothing we purchase and decide to wear projects and promotes a certain message about us.

Creating an image of how we will be perceived by others is highly impacted by our use of social media. Just think of how easy it is to open up Instagram and scroll through your favorite style influencers' profiles to discover the latest trends and most-hyped beauty products. We have unlimited access to all the content put forth by models, fashion influencers, and celebrities so it can be difficult to determine what is actually relevant for us.

Robin Givhan has been commenting on the fashion industry's thematic narratives and cultural references for over twenty years. If the goal of a writer is to share her views while simultaneously provoking independent thought in readers, then Robin Givhan is certainly doing a good job at that. Givhan points out the cracks in American culture and fashion's failure to speak up about racial and social injustices. And it's not just remarking on every story with the turn of the news cycle, but fashion's need to preserve the idea of The American Dream.[51]

Fashion as Protest: VSTRO

If Neo-Nazis are able to turn to fashion as a way to normalize their beliefs and values, who is to say that fashion can't also be used also to protest? While the alt-right turns to fashion as a propaganda tool, political activists have also effectively found ways to champion their causes through fashion.

Jordan LeRoy links West Coast fashion with hip hop to combat racism and hatred.[57] He started AstroKnots, which brought together artists working toward a common goal across all sorts of artistic mediums, but primarily hip hop.[57] This network of musical artists didn't exactly take off like he had hoped, but the experience gave him a solid foundation. When he realized that people were energized by the idea of music and fashion, he launched VSTRO to show pride in hip hop culture.[57]

When designing VSTRO, LeRoy focused on not only developing a line far superior to most in fit, comfort, and style but also in reflecting a greater subculture of Western hip hop. "I combine multiple styles together with popular streetwear trends, which breathes fresh life into street fashion world, in my opinion. Furthermore, all of our products are made by hand, from scratch, by our cut and sew partners," says LeRoy.[57] All of his products debuted following Charlottesville, and feature messaging of "FVCK RACISM."[57]

According to LeRoy, "The FVCK RACISM movement stands in direct opposition to racism everywhere. Not just against African Americans. Not just in America. We are an inclusive movement ready to represent the human race as a whole. The entire world needs to adopt this ideology and eradicate the acknowledgment of skin tone differentiation completely. This is an accomplishable goal if we all stand together, united, and refuse to back down until it is accomplished. As a movement we actually intend to do just that. Move forward—specifically, in the direction of a better, more compassionate, and understanding world," he says.[57] The VSTRO brand is about more than just trendy streetwear-inspired t-shirts. VSTRO actually works toward achieving this goal of equality. Over a Christmas, LeRoy and his crew spent hours distributing donations to the homeless who were stuck out in the cold.[57]

LeRoy's philosophy on activism through fashion is quite simple. "Upon the creation of my brand, I decided that I wanted my clothing to represent something more than just a brand. When I sat down to think about it, I realized that the clothes we wear are essentially billboards advertising our personalities and our beliefs," he says.[57] "When I came to this realization, I uncovered the true power that a clothing brand can possess. A brand can be a foundational platform, which provides stability for the artist looking to share a sincere message with the world. The creators of a brand can use their platform to spread a message, whether positive or negative, to the furthest reaches of society—to places not as easily reached by other industries. For VSTRO, that activism has taken shape in the form of activism against racism and mental illness awareness, as well as serving as a beacon of encouragement for all those who seek to manifest a dream into reality. We seek to inspire the dreamers and the believers, the thinkers and the achievers. I guess you could say I want to be the spark that ignites the flame."[57]

Protest Messaging

Heather Picquot heads the culture section of trend forecasting agency Fashion Snoops, in New York City. She identifies the major macro-cultural trends that influence consumers.[52] Nowadays, it's all about Gen Z and millennials.

In order to appeal to these groups, Heather and her team determine what these consumers really care about. Gen Z and millennials are passionate about taking a stand for what they believe in and supporting brands that align with their values. In order to grab their attention, brands need an authentic messaging platform to align themselves with causes they believe in.[58]

Itay Arad, CEO of Fashion Snoops, says that the main reason the company succeeds is because employees are continually identifying and monitoring macro trends so their predictions are never a shot in the dark.[59] Fashion Snoops observes how cultural trends develop over time and determines how they translate into design inspiration. They gather insight and inspiration from observing these cultural shifts.

On a mass-market level, protest messages on t-shirts have been extremely influential in promoting certain causes and grabbing the attention of millennial and Gen Z consumers. What actually constitutes authentic messaging on these popular political statement t-shirts? How can we ensure that the messaging on the shirt is a genuine call to action and not just a latest trend?[58]

The Dior "We should all be feminists" shirt that gained popularity in 2017 is a solid example of genuine messaging to support a real cause.[60] Heather Picquot says the shirt "was a powerful statement because it was right around the time of the first Women's March and the reaction to Trump being elected."[58] And Maria Grazia Chiuri was the first woman to hold the creative director position at Dior.[60] But are other brands following in Dior's footsteps to blaze a trail of genuine messaging in fashion? Do brands really care?

* * *

Brand and culture should align, argues Denise Lee Yohn in her book, *Fusion: How Integrating Brand and Culture Powers the World's Greatest Companies.*[61] Yohn writes that companies need to take an inside-out approach and integrate their brand with the whole company's experience, including employees as well as customers.[61]

Trends are constantly changing and evolving, and Fashion Snoops is at the forefront of forecasting and analyzing trends. Fashion Snoops uses data and media stories to see which content receives the most coverage and then aligns it to product and analyzes its success. "I think the longevity of a trend is rooted in lifestyle," Heather tells me to show that trends are not just about latest fads, but are heavily influenced by the past.[58]

In Heather's opinion, it is possible to take authentic messaging to the next level to spur broader social change. "I think people are okay with aligning yourself with an organization in the proper way and then using it on your t-shirts," she admits.[58] In 2017, Patagonia became the first retailer to withdraw from a major trade show as a statement of protection of public land.[62] Maria Grazia Chiuri's "we are all feminists" t-shirt is, according to Heather, a great statement of undoubtable authenticity.[58]

By aligning brands with the right causes, fashion gains even more power and influence, becoming an effective platform for leveraging social change. Brands like ASOS Made in Kenya, which produces ethical fashion in support of social issues like unemployment and AIDS, prove that the cause doesn't end with the messaging on a t-shirt.[63] In fact, it is just the beginning.

Building Your Tribe

Vanessa de Lisle served as fashion editor for *Harper's & Queen* and British *Vogue* before launching a career as a stylist and fashion consultant.[64] Vanessa explains that she believes "one of the biggest mistakes brands make is that they think they want to please everyone. You can't please everyone. You have to choose your market."[64] She says that successful retailers need to focus on their tribe, a term she uses to describe a brand's specific target audience.[64]

* * *

Alex Batdorf is a serial entrepreneur on a mission to disrupt the fashion industry. After founding her company ZipFit Denim, which provides customers with the best-fitting, customized designer denim, Alex has moved on to coach and empower female entrepreneurs to "get shit done!"[65] She pushes young entrepreneurs to be authentic and true to themselves. She asks entrepreneurs to ponder, "What am I losing by not showing up as me?"[65]

It is important to stand in your purpose in everything you do. Alex says that once you find your purpose, the question then becomes: What can I do today that will allow me to feel my impact? Every little thing you do should impact your purpose and answer the question of why.[65]

Alex, like Vanessa de Lisle, articulates the importance of building a strong tribe of mentors.[65] Success comes to those who invest the time and effort in cultivating a strong tribe of people they can rely on.

Alex has always been interested in using clothing as a tool to amplify how she feels and authentically express herself. Alex says fashion can express whatever message you want to convey. For her, style is reflective of her interests and elevates her mood.[65] She never dresses down, always making an effort to look pulled together.

I totally agree with Alex. I also use fashion to bring myself out of a slump or bad mood. When I was an inpatient at a rehabilitation center in New Jersey, my parents bought me t-shirts with uplifting messages to wear as I learned to dress myself. Shirts with phrases like "Positive Vibes Only" and "(Do)n't Qu(it)" were thrown into circulation. Wearing clothing that shared a positive message greatly impacted my mood. I found myself coming to accept and believe in the messages on my t-shirts. It's unbelievable how quickly the positive vibes would take root and spread throughout the hospital. I found all the patients and workers were always quick to lift each other up. I think that fashion brands that can embrace authenticity and effectively convey their passion and purpose to customers will be the most successful.

What to Watch for:

- Young fashion innovators and consumers gaining influence and demanding their voices be heard
- Increasing irrelevance of the traditional fashion trend cycle—consumers continue to gravitate toward clothes that can be worn in any season.
- Continued brand alignment with consumer values
- Increasing integrated retail experience and brands further honing and scaling direct-to-consumer models
- Media is becoming the store, and stores are becoming outlets for brands to provide a unique retail experience for customers
- No longer what you sell but how you sell
- A growing movement similar to the Civil Rights Movement in the sixties, of consumers turning to fashion as a tool to express their own message and version of themselves
- Fashion is being used as a tool to promote varying political agendas for better or worse
- an authentic message through their clothing that appeals to their audience
- More fashion brands turning toward activism to align themselves with social issues and raise awareness
- Consumers embracing individuality by using fashion as a tool for self-expression

PART 4

YOUNG INNOVATORS

A definite shift toward younger innovators making waves characterizes the changing fashion landscape. Young entrepreneurs in fashion today care about connecting with their consumers and building a community to directly engage with them. Branded communities are unique in that they invite consumers to participate in an experience. I believe this concept transforms consumer expectations to anticipate all-encompassing interactions with their favorite brands. It's not enough anymore for brands to simply promote their product; consumers expect them to be accompanied by an integrated retail experience.

Brand Promotion

Jake Hart understands the importance of successful marketing campaigns to launch a fashion business. In high school, Jake had the idea to combine picturesque elements of mountains, beaches, and suburban life and put them on high-quality t-shirts. So he started a clothing company, Idyllic.[66] But that was the easy part. Jake worked hard to spread the word about his simplistic lifestyle brand.

"When I started it, it was like this really unattainable dream, but then when I began I realized it really wasn't that far-fetched," Jake shares.[66] But while launching a brand that promoted the values of the beach, skating, and suburban life itself wasn't too hard, finding unique ways to promote his brand proved difficult. One big surprise came in the form of skateboarder Liam Morgan, who wore an Idyllic tee in his video.[66]

Affiliation with prominent names in the skateboarding space elevated the brand's presence. Idyllic even managed to secure a collaboration with Aéropostale, which sold thousands of Jake's t-shirts in stores worldwide.[66]

Creating Community

SoulCycle grew wildly successful due to the community it created, combining fitness with mental health. On the BoF Voices stage, CEO Melanie Whelan discussed SoulCycle's growth and how the company plans to scale to reach even greater heights by building its community.

Since its founding in 2006, SoulCycle has expanded from one initial studio in the Upper East Side to eighty-five studios across the country, led by committed instructors who love what they do. "It's all about our people," said Whelan.[67] "Our product is experience and our experience is created by people."[67] SoulCycle instructors are the key to the brand's incredible success. The three hundred-plus instructors across the nation cultivate and promote the company's special culture and environment.[67]

Whelan understands the need for providing quality care and benefits for SoulCycle instructors in order to attract and retain highly qualified and enthusiastic trainers who will spread the SoulCycle message and motivate riders.[67] "The fitness industry has typically been very fragmented in how they approach talent," said Whelan.[60] "[Instructors] were more worried about their schedules and where their next pay check was coming from versus building a community. So we've created a space for instructors to really focus on building community."[67]

"That ethos and that drive has kept us going for the last eleven years—making sure our hospitality is on point, that our experience is on point," said Whelan. "We are only as good as our last ride."[67]

Fashion can take a lesson from SoulCycle and the immense success the brand has achieved by cultivating a community of motivated and like-minded people. By gravitating toward a direct-to-consumer model approach, brands can ensure meaningful engagement with consumers.

Spreading a Positive Brand Message

Joshua Sitt is a 2018 Georgetown grad and one of the creative geniuses behind streetwear label, Madhappy, which aims to embody and spread a message of positivity and inclusion as a lifestyle brand that interacts with and directly engages customers.

Madhappy was originally created as a way for the founders to channel their creative frustration. After a year-long hiatus from the fashion industry following minimal success with another fashion brand, the Madhappy founders knew they needed to do something differently. They wanted to create something fun, so they began by exclusively working with friends and family.

"The beauty of Madhappy is that each person can have their own interpretation of it. In our opinion, Madhappy is the essence of life: two words coming together to create a life-like existence. It's about the ups and downs and everything in between. It is recognizing that everything isn't perfect because it shouldn't be. It is realizing that the lows make the highs that much more pronounced. It is seeing that the obstacles in life are actually what life is truly about. The path, the journey, the struggle, help illuminate the very fact to us that the obstacle is the way. We must pursue a better version of ourselves and the world around us while still recognizing that everything is fine just as it is. Sometimes we're mad. Sometimes we're happy. However, in spite of all of this, or maybe because of it, we can always be Madhappy," say the founders.[68]

One of Madhappy's main goals is to establish a community around the brand. By engaging directly with customers on social media, the Madhappy crew is able to get product feedback quickly. Josh tells me Madhappy is more than just clothing.[69] Madhappy constantly puts forth an authentic brand experience for its customers, from SoulCycle classes to art exhibits in their pop-up shops in Aspen, Brooklyn, or Miami.[69] Madhappy is all about customer engagement.

"It also gives millennials a new and more acceptable way to express their emotions through trend," Josh says.[69] The Madhappy success story is a prime example of a clothing brand that has expanded beyond product to offer consumers an immersive retail experience. Madhappy dutifully connects with followers to get feedback and promote new events.[69] A main focus is on collaborating with different charities and forming new partnerships to host events for their fans. The goal is to spread the Madhappy message, which people can experience through the brand's social media and special events.[69]

Madhappy hosted a collaboration with both ModelFIT and SoulCycle to spread the message of positivity and mental health.[69] By hosting workout classes and charity events, Madhappy demonstrates its focus on building a lifestyle brand over the clothing. Josh tells me the company's goal is to encompass this positive message and cross boundaries to new areas, exploring styles people have never tested before.[69] He wants to do something to stand out. For example, the brand's signature hand-stitched detail on the hoods of sweatshirts has proved to be a key feature that fans love.

The brand also focuses on spreading a message of positivity and inclusivity through the clothing's bold colors and designs. One of the brand's newer premises on butterflies emphasizes equality.[69]

Antidote X

Much like Joshua Sitt, Paolo Moreno, founder of streetwear label Antidote X, seeks to leverage his brand as a platform to encourage others to pursue their passions.[70] After starting the clothing line with his friend Pedro, Paolo told me he wanted to use this opportunity to inspire others with an interest in fashion. "I want people to get out of their seats and do something," Moreno said.[70] "Create and impel. I've inspired a lot of individuals to start their own brands or even just buy their own camera to photograph. Art is a language, and I want to incentivize creativity."[70]

Madhappy and Antidote X effectively capitalize on the inclusive community movement, laying the groundwork for other brands to join. An article in *The Week* expanded on the influence that reviews have on consumers looking to purchase from any given store.[71] A 2017 survey revealed that consumers look to online sites for information reviews on local businesses and trust these online reviews almost as much as personal recommendations.[72]

This community of consumers who participate in the review culture has a mass impact on both businesses and consumers. Since positive reviews hugely impact potential consumers, they can help smaller businesses compete with bigger brands. These reviews level the playing field between chains and independent businesses, says Brett Hollenback, an assistant professor at the UCLA Anderson School of Management.[72]

Consumers increasingly rely on positive and negative online reviews. It doesn't so much matter if the review is positive or negative, what matters to consumers is that there *is* a review. A community of customers around a culture of reviews will only continue to influence the purchase decision-making process in the next few years.

What to Watch for:

- The shift toward increasingly younger entrepreneurs as major innovators in fashion—younger people have the pulse on street culture and the most relevant trends.
- Fashion labels shifting focus from exclusive product promotion to an inclusive and integrated retail experience for customers
- More brands beginning to latch on to the community and experience model SoulCycle so effectively employs
- Brands supporting causes like mental health and as a result attracting new consumers
- Consumers' increased reliance of online reviews to influence choices

PART 5

PAST INFLUENCE ON NEW TRENDS

"I am interested in the idea of humanism that nourishes creativity. The human connection that forms this Maison is for me the best team possible. Here I have discovered that no innovation can exist without a profound knowledge of tradition. At the same time, I know that the sense of limit that springs from this awareness gives you the freedom of thinking of how to trespass it. This, in synthesis, will be the new Valentino direction. A human narration, personal yet unanimous, of a story that is yet to be written."

—PIERPAOLO PICCIOLI, CREATIVE DIRECTOR, VALENTINO

Juicy Couture

The Business of Fashion published an article on Juicy Couture's rise to fame and attempt at a fashion renaissance built on nostalgia. "Nostalgia has proven to be one of our brand's greatest assets," wrote the company's creative director Jamie Mizrahi, "and I truly believe it will be the springboard to launch us into the next phase of the brand's evolution."[73] Mizrahi asserts that in the age of athleisure, the Juicy tracksuit has proven it can evolve with the times.

Juicy's first runway show, held in the Hotel Wolcott in New York City, featured a wide array of reinvented Juicy tracksuits. We saw velvety tracksuits, as well as tie dyed and striped numbers.[74] Mizrahi was a teenager during the time of Juicy Couture's rise to fame in the early 2000s, and she can remember the exact time she purchased her first tracksuit and the impact it had on her. "It was waffle material and it was oatmeal colored and I thought I was the coolest person ever for having it," she told a fashion blog.[73]

In 2015, the Victoria and Albert Museum in London acquired a pepto-pink version of an original Juicy tracksuit, reasserting the tracksuit's cultural relevance.[73] And now the brand is attempting a nostalgia renaissance, considering the generation that grew up lusting after Dior bags and Fila slides is finally reaching financial maturity.

When Juicy first launched in 2001, it was one of the first brands to popularize the high-end tracksuit.[68] While this may not seem that big of a deal given our current landscape of high-end athleisure, from Virgil Off-White tees to Yeezy Calabasa sweats, arguably Juicy Couture first spurred this high-end athleisure movement. The Juicy tracksuit was just pricey enough to be revered as a symbol of status, yet attainable enough for teens across the country to add multiple pairs to their wardrobes.

The tracksuit radiates comfort and style. The trashy chic appeal of the Juicy Couture tracksuit was first popularized by Paris Hilton, the first celebrity to wear her tracksuit on the red carpet, paired with her Louis Vuitton and Fendi bags.[69]

Suddenly, Juicy Couture became cool, and the tracksuit was transformed by celebrity status into one of the most lusted-after articles of clothing. Paris Hilton's rise to fame changed the way consumers viewed high fashion and the tracksuit. Hilton realized early on "that the concept of celebrity in the digital era was shifting, and that the new aristocracy would be determined not by talent or tastefulness but by the ability to exploit attention."[76]

It really didn't matter where the tracksuit was worn or in what context. What mattered was that you were *seen* wearing it. Juicy founders were reported to keep a wall in their office filled with photos of people wearing Juicy Couture to any number of situations—from a walk in the park to grocery shopping.[76] Murderess Patrizia Reggiani was even rumored to have worn Juicy to the funeral of her ex-husband. It later came out that she was actually clad in Gucci, but the details are irrelevant.[69] What matters is that the tracksuit shot to a level of superior status and consumers were changing the narrative around where the product could be worn.

"The original tracksuits thrived at a time before the mainstreaming of the body-positivity movement, and founders Nash-Taylor and Skaist-Levy proudly used their own petite frames as sample sizes for the garments, which were designed to bare just a hint of tanned, toned midriff. In the early days, they advised their seamstresses to skew small: 'If you think they look like baby clothes, they are the right size.'"[77]

And today, the reemergence of the Juicy tracksuit puts forth a very different message than the petite and trashy aesthetic of the two thousands. Elle Fanning wore a pink new Mizrahi creation and looked comfy and relaxed in a way that previous generations of Juicy fanatics hadn't.[78] The tracksuits of today are less conducive for belly button baring, more conducive for exuding a vibe of leisure and extreme comfort.

Celebrities like Britney Spears who helped popularize the Juicy look, seem to have reservations about its reemergence to relive its heyday. The fact of the matter is that Juicy is no longer the only brand that caters toward the athleisure market.[75] In fact, if the company wants to be perceived as relevant and influential in the space, it will need to play catch-up to the big players in athleisure first.

* * *

This trend in nostalgia-influenced fashion is perhaps most obvious through the logomania craze. This obsession with logos can be seen through the re-emergence of the John Galliano-era obsession with the Dior logo saddlebag or anything Gucci.

But what explains this nostalgic resurgence of logo-infused products? I think that apart from the fact that the nineties culture comeback continues, the simple truth is that logos look good on Instagram. For consumers eager to impress upon their followers an image of high fashion and thoughtful personal style, logos really resonate.

Fashion Snoops Trend Analysis

Fashion Snoops focuses less on fast trends, and more so on catering to a very specific customer, one who knows what kind of style she likes and wants.

Fashion Snoops scores all areas for inspiration. For example, a color like millennial pink will trend for a hot second, but there will always be colors like navy and black that stay relevant regardless of season. "It's not like the whole world will subscribe to a trendy new color," says Heather Picquot.[79] About every ten years, we revisit the trends of the past and try to find new ways to put a modern twist on them.

For example, Gen Z and millennials are obsessed with the nineties. Walk into an Urban Outfitters, and it looks like a blast from the (recent) past. Gen Z loves that teenager look: Brandy Melville crop tops, high-waisted jeans, Vans sneakers. They're obsessed with 2004 Britney Spears, so it's only fitting that Britney is the face of Kenzo.[80]

It's hard to know per se the lifespan of trends and what is in and what is out, but cultural indicators definitely help. Skinny jeans and off-the-shoulder tops aren't exactly the hottest thing right now but they're not unstylish. People still wear them all the time and find ways to incorporate them with trendy new pieces to modernize an outfit.

And speaking of nostalgia in fashion, many Gen Z and millennials today barely know where the stuff they're obsessed with originated. Much of their understanding comes from research on Tumblr and other social media channels.[79]

"The runway six years ago used to be important. Today, we

look more toward street style. While runway trends are still relevant, the way in which consumers engage with these looks is changing. You don't need to sit front row at a fashion show. You can watch it on your computer. It's no longer that top-down Holy Grail of fashion," Heather muses.[79] Analyzing street style is big but also data, Pinterest, and Google search trends.

Inspiration for future trends comes from all over the world, and forecasting agencies like Fashion Snoops are already predicting trends two to three years in advance. Fashion Snoops looks a lot to data that the world provides. Trends in how we live and where we are heading were never investigated in forecasting before, but "it's just all so connected," Heather adds.[79]

What to Watch For:

- Reinventions of old tracksuit favorites continue to make waves in the dynamic and evolving athleisure market
- An athleisure revolution rooted in a nostalgic nod to the past
- More brands looking to past trends for tomorrow's fashion inspiration
- Increasing relevance of current events and pop culture in forecasting trends

PART 6

DIVERSITY

It is no secret that fashion's relationship with race has been, for the most part, one-sided. The very structure of the fashion industry promotes exclusion. Talk of Industry insiders today focuses on the lack of proper representation of traditionally excluded and under-represented communities of people.

At the Fashion Snoops Trend Immersion Day I attended in May 2018, highlighting the cultural mega trends influencing the next few seasons, the opening speaker addressed these concerns. Savon Bartley is a world-renowned spoken-word poet, writer, and teacher with a passion for storytelling. He opened the day's event with a special poem he wrote to set the tone of the day. "The future is representation," he spoke to a captive audience.[81] "The future is a fire we will create together."

How appropriate that our introduction to a day of macro-cultural trends began with such a powerful statement. Fashion is certainly taking steps toward creating more inclusive communities, ensuring that people from all walks of life are represented. In these chapters I explore the developments in this inclusion movement.

Consider the clear industry bias toward young, thin models. The voices of aging women are starting to rise to the spotlight, dispelling misconceptions around age and relevance. This movement of older women aims to subvert false notions of what it looks and feels like to be old. The most interesting part is that the majority of the following is younger women. "We lived in extraordinary times," says seventy-one-year old Australian artist, Jenny Kee. "These girls know that. They know what we lived through. They envy us."[82]

The Future of Luxury and the Need for Increased Industry Diversity

The Juicy Couture nostalgia renaissance emphasizes the importance of digitalization to advertise a genuine brand message that directly relates to consumer values. The appointment of Virgil Abloh as menswear creative director at Louis Vuitton got everyone buzzing about the future of his own brand and luxury fashion. The founder of streetwear label Off White and Creative Director for Kanye West does not have formal training in fashion yet managed to start his own successful youth-culture-focused streetwear brand. And Virgil is the first black man to hold the menswear creative director position for the French heritage house.[83]

Abloh's appointment has great implications for the future of fashion and luxury. The industry is waking up to the importance of employing a diverse body of talent in positions of leadership at major fashion houses. Virgil Abloh's strong focus on streetwear and youth culture undoubtedly influences his creativity and innovation at Louis Vuitton. Stavros Karelis stated in an interview with *Hypebeast* that, "with the vast amount of work that [Virgil] has produced in the recent years with his Off-White brand, [he proves] that he talks to a very wide spectrum of audience with a cultural and political message always attached to his work. His collaborations and choice of different mediums to express his work have been extremely popular in a way that very few have managed in recent times. The young generation adores him and the older generation cannot help but admire not only the end product but the dialogue and social impact he generates."[84]

Is Virgil Abloh's appointment a push to bring Louis Vuitton into the twenty-first century with streetwear? Virgil Abloh undoubtedly reaches a wide audience. He has the pulse on youth street culture and melds it together with a luxury element. While critics claim his designs are overpriced and uninspired, supporters think he has found a way to profit that could really have an impact at Louis Vuitton. He is also only the third black man ever to receive an appointment to a major French fashion heritage house.[85]

Abloh acknowledges the barriers to entry in fashion and strives to break those down. "I have to prove that this is design, that this is art, that this is valid," he told *W Magazine*.[85]

What's more, he appeals to a generation that may appreciate streetwear, but doesn't consider streetwear designers as being at the level of their peers. Abloh has repeatedly made a point to be part of the newer wave of innovators, surrounding himself with teens and twenty-somethings. Identifying with them has long been one of his top priorities: "I'm always trying to prove to my seventeen-year-old self that I can do creative things I thought weren't possible," he says.[86] This attitude has already positively impacted his creativity at Louis Vuitton.

As the artistic director of Louis Vuitton's menswear collections, Abloh stepped into the role vacated by his friend and mentor Kim Jones. "It is an honor for me to accept this position. I find the heritage and creative integrity of the house are key inspirations and will look to reference them both while drawing parallels to modern times," he says in a statement.[86] He has clearly demonstrated his desire to open up the industry to create opportunities for designers and people of color.

Fashion shouldn't be skewed to favor those with privileged backgrounds. It should be open to whoever wishes to contribute, and Virgil has made it his mission to break down those barriers to entry for underserved communities. While he certainly needs to prove himself in this role, you can be sure he will bring his passion for equality to Louis Vuitton.

Rise of Luxury Streetwear

"I feel like Raf Simons is important for the culture based on the fact that he built a whole new religion around fashion. It's to the point where kids, male and female alike, will get in full arguments over why he's the greatest. And it's amazing how his prior work, his archive, is more important and relevant than anything that's out today. When you wrap your mind around the concept that he wrote the future of fashion and design in the 1990s and early 2000s, you'll also understand why Raf is the greatest to ever do it," says Rakim Mayers, more commonly known by his stage name, A$AP Rocky.[87]

In the interview, Rocky references the cultural relevance and ubiquity of high fashion in hip hop. An article by Christopher Morency for *The Business of Fashion* emphasizes the new reality that rappers are fashion's royalty.[88] "It's important for this generation and the next generation to see people who look like them or that inspire them because fashion isn't just for the elite anymore," says A$AP Rocky in the interview.[88]

Rocky has worked hard over the past decade to establish himself as a cultural icon in the world of high fashion and luxury while maintaining a strong hip hop presence.[89] Rocky is just as well known by youth for his sense of style as he is for his music.

In a sense, A$AP Rocky brought cultish high fashion to the masses. Gucci and Louis Vuitton are household names. Not everyone can afford to buy into the high fashion hype, but there is a strong cultural awareness associated with these brands.

Not everyone so far removed from the fashion world knows about Raf Simons and his immense influence on menswear. Frank Ocean calls out Simons' fashion in his verse of A$AP Mob song, "Raf: I covered my face and I'm bloody / That's Spring/Summer 2002."[90] This more abstract reference to the garments worn by models in Simons' 2002 collection demonstrates Rocky's extensive fashion knowledge. While many rappers do not hesitate to flex their high fashion to the public, few flex their knowledge of designers and "Fashion Killa" status quite like A$AP Rocky does.

"Fashion is for everyone, and the more you try to exclude people, you'll find out that those are the same people you need to include the most," he says in an interview.[87] This tendency for rappers to engage with high fashion and luxury speaks to a larger macro trend blurring the lines between fashion and art, and it redefines their propensity for individuality and creative self-expression. Many credit Kanye West as being one of the first to blur gender norms through fashion and pave the way for the next generation of rappers. When he wore a Celine womenswear blouse to Coachella, he made a statement on conventional ideas around masculinity.[91] As much as some may criticize Kanye's music, there is no denying his supreme influence on street style. His status as a visionary in music and fashion allows him to ultimately influence and educate younger generations.

And the youth are listening. Kanye's much anticipated Adidas/Yeezy collab did not disappoint, captivating the interest of many a young, street-savvy Gen Zer. We are living in an interesting time, where the factors driving the latest trends are changing along with the people who popularize them. Gucci and Balenciaga have come to be associated more with pop culture-savvy teens than traditionally affluent middle-aged women. Hip hop and social media drive the latest trends and influence which brands are associated with them.

How can we explain the luxury streetwear trend? Teens these days are obsessed with streetwear labels like Supreme, Vans, and Adidas. Demand for clothing and shoes that project that classic street vibe has absolutely skyrocketed in recent years. Erinn Murphy, senior research analyst at Piper Jaffray, shared with *BoF* that "both Vans and Adidas have this 'open-source' platform where they allow pop culture to help guide and influence how they are positioned with the consumer today. Having a very collaborative environment when it comes to the softer side of brands is very important."[92]

Luxe Digital reported that by 2025, 45 percent of the global luxury market is expected to be millennials.[84] Gucci told *Forbes* that about 50 percent of the company's sales come from millennial consumers.[93] And that number will only continue to rise as awareness of high fashion increases.

Inclusivity Movement

One of the most notable and prominent forms of misrepresentation that highlights the industry's problem is around blackness. H&M lost its partnership with R&B singer/songwriter, The Weeknd, after the brand put forth an ad that featured an African American boy wearing a sweatshirt with the words "coolest monkey in the jungle."[94] The Weeknd tweeted to his eight million+ followers that he would no longer work with the company as he was so offended by the ad campaign.[94]

But it will take more than inclusive ad campaigns to appeal to consumers when so many brands consistently fail to acknowledge the diversity of their audience.

Gucci received criticism for advertising turbans that resemble those worn by the Sikh community.[95] What added to the controversy was that the models who wore these controversial turbans were all white.[95] Wouldn't the authencity of ethnic—or religious-inspired—clothing be enhanced if the models represented the target audience?

* * *

Inclusive ad campaigns extend beyond the need for proper representation of religious groups. For example, blackness has historically been misrepresented and appropriated in fashion. "Generally speaking, blackness and some of its attendant vernaculars of representation have been white-washed and then made highly visible in serving to enhance mainstream fashion styles with a 'street' or 'urban' or 'ghetto (fabulous)' avant garde edgy lefty revolutionary ethnic aesthetic," explains Laura Harris, Professor in Africana studies at Pitzer College.[96]

In 2016, model Nykhor Paul published a statement to her Instagram account that she was "tired of apologizing for [her] blackness."[97] Always expected to provide her own makeup at shoots, Nykhor Paul tired of makeup artists inexperienced at applying to her complexion struggle to do her makeup. And yet all the other models (most of them white) just showed up to the shoot, greeted by professional artists ready to apply the makeup without all the fuss. It seems to me that fashion brands should employ makeup artists for their shows who are experienced and knowledgeable about applying makeup to all different skin types and looks. It would be a worthwhile investment, after all, as runways continue to diversify. Consumers will expect to see more relatable faces.

* * *

And yet, unfortunately the inclusivity issue in fashion extends far beyond the reaches of models and their makeup artists. Fashion magazines still see their fair share of discrimination in the workplace. When Edward Enninful was appointed as editor of British *Vogue*, model activist Naomi Campbell called it "a historic moment."[98] Historic indeed it was, as he is the first black man to be appointed to such a high position in a fashion magazine, but I hope for the day where appointments such as Enninful's aren't viewed as seminal or historic but rather as normal. Significant measures have been taken to address the lack of diversity in fashion, but fashion really needs to revamp its efforts to include and appeal to an increasingly diverse audience.

Inclusion applies beyond racial equality and acceptance. Consider this stat—by 2040, Islam is set to surpass Judaism as the second most prominent religion in the United States.[99] Times are changing, and its time fashion hops on board and adapts to its changing consumer demographic.

Some people already are. Fashion blogger Valerie Eguavoen of the popular blog *On a Curve,* called out the online designer boutique *Revolve* for its lack of model diversity on a press trip to Thailand. She didn't hesitate to share her thoughts on her blog: "Hey @Revolve, while I absolutely love @songofstyle and some of the girls from your crew, I have a question. Where is the diversity? You mean to tell me that the lifestyle/beauty/fashion influencers you include in your projects cannot have a certain amount of melanin?"[100]

Eguavoen says she decided to address the issue head-on because she felt the brand wouldn't do it. So someone had to. "I feel it is my duty as a member of any society to disrupt any system that normalizes discrimination," she says in an interview.[100] And this problem is bigger than *Revolve.* This is a deeply rooted problem of systemic racism that normalizes racial discrimination.

Shortly after this call-out, Song of Style blogger Aimee Song responded to Eguavoen's post. She defended Revolve, saying that the company has one of the more diverse teams of fashion brands she has worked with.[101] She wasn't endorsing the photos but figured that the reason for this lack of diversity was because there aren't enough known or famous influencers to draw from. This angered Eguavoen, who launched the You Belong Now campaign to raise awareness of influencers of color in fashion and increase their visibility.[101]

Laura Harris elaborates further on this unbalanced relationship between fashion and race. She explains that for the longest time, fashion has basically paid lip service to diversity without actually tackling the issue of representation head-on.[96] It can't be argued that the runways have become more inclusive over the past few seasons, but the question remains: is this push for diversity more a reactionary attempt to save face than a genuine push for proper representation?

Importance of Knowing Your Audience: Diversity in Beauty/Makeup

However, is the heightened visibility of issues of representation in beauty and fashion purely a commercial ploy, or is there actual substance behind this progression? The improvements in representation from the design and modeling side reflect the industry's tokenistic approach to race.

For example, one aspect of Virgil Abloh's appointment to menswear creative director of Louis Vuitton demonstrates progress toward more consistent inclusion of under-represented peoples, but on the other hand, the question remains as to whether or not his appointment was commercially driven or a true sign of acceptance. "Nobody at that level of fashion has to talk about race or politics if they don't want to, and I don't think Virgil Abloh is any different in that regard," fashion writer Melvin Backman tells *Hypebeast*.[102] Expecting Abloh to yield a social and political agenda without holding white designers to the same standards is just hypocritical.

"The industry must move toward fully embracing and supporting talent, without bias. Without inclusion, collectively, especially from the behind the scenes, a glass ceiling will remain for independent entrepreneurs and designers who are black," says designer Victor Glemaud, a finalist in the CFDA/ Vogue Fashion Fund.[103]

For diverse appointments of designers of color to positions of power in the industry to amount to any lasting impact, it will be essential to get beyond the surface-level hype of a designer's name to establish real, socially driven visions.

What to Watch For:

- A continued shift to a more inclusive fashion
- Emergence of more designers and models of color into positions of power in fashion
- More brands channeling the influence of youth culture into clothing
- A move away from a tokenistic approach to diversity in fashion and a push for more diverse and inclusive appointments
- A continued spike in streetwear culture, sparked by today's youth
- Mix of luxury with streetwear, further pushing the boundaries on what constitutes high fashion

- Heightened visibility of people of color in all aspects of the fashion industry
- Fashion embracing diversity in beauty and clothing lines

PART 7

ACCESSIBLE FASHION

"Inclusivity and the democratization of fashion have always been at the core of my brand's DNA. These collections continue to build on that vision, empowering differently abled adults to express themselves through fashion."

—TOMMY HILFIGER[104]

In 2010, it was reported that 19 percent, or 56.7 million Americans, claimed to have a disability. That number only increases with each year.[105] The study, "The Future of Disability in America," posits that the number of Americans living with limitations will increase over the coming years if nothing is done to accommodate their mobility and activity limitations.[106]

Fashion Activism in Action

Fashion activist Sinéad Burke understands firsthand the need for fashion companies to embrace brand inclusivity. Born with achondroplasia and standing at a height of 3.5 feet tall, Sinéad has struggled with clothes shopping her entire life.[107] For her, it is virtually impossible to find clothing that fits her short limbs and upper body.

According to Sinéad, there are 1.2 billion disabled people in the world when you combine physical and mental impairments.[107] That's a lot of people. It is time for brands to change their mindset and develop clothing with consumers of all abilities in mind.

Sinéad also touches on the need to acknowledge and amplify the voices of the disabled community. "They've not been invited to the table to help make and share decisions," Sinéad tells *The Business of Fashion*.[107] Her fashion activism raises awareness of the issues disabled people face on a daily basis, and she encourages brands to create with these consumers in mind.

A 2013 report on The Global Economics of Disability calculated that the 1.2 billion disabled people in the world have a combined annual disposable income of 1 trillion.[98] And then if you factor in this group's friends and family, it adds another 6.9 trillion dollars. Sinéad focuses on bridging the gap between vulnerable groups and fashion executives. She can understand and relate with the fashion struggle.

Sinéad says "one of the challenges of fashion is that it is notoriously hierarchical, and it profits from exclusivity. In order for the disabled market to be relevant and to have their voices validated, there must be power sharing. Very few people within the fashion industry in positions of power have experience or empathy within this arena. If they design for difference without a tangible understanding, the product becomes patronizing. Or it comes about that we think only in terms of function."[107] By inviting disabled people to the join the fashion conversation, we will certainly be better equipped to create practical fashion designs for people of all abilities.

Fashion definitely profits from exclusion and status, but shouldn't brands jump on this growth opportunity and expand to reach more consumers who have traditionally been neglected?

Consider something as simple as a zipper on a jacket. My whole life, I have been able to throw on and zip up my jackets with ease. Now, I find myself dependent on someone else to zip up the garment for me as my left-hand struggles to grip the jacket and zipper.

You can bet I've learned some neat tricks for buttoning and zipping with one hand, but it is still very difficult. And like

Sinéad, I know I am not the only person who faces these issues. Clothes that are considered fashionable are simply not designed for consumers with disabilities in mind, I've learned. With all the thousands of people out there facing issues with getting dressed, you would think brands would embrace this opportunity to attract new customers. So why is this not always seen as the case?

Clothes shopping is hard, and even harder when you have physical limitations in dressing yourself. Model Mama Cax admits, "I often have to alter things myself," as it is difficult to find clothing that can accommodate her prosthetic.[109] Keah Brown writes in an article for *Glamour* that disabled people are constantly reminded that they do not belong, especially regarding fashion.[110] She writes that Rebecca Cokley, a senior fellow at the Center for American Progress and a little person, estimates paying double for all her clothes once she factors in the cost of alterations.[110] And shopping in the kids' section is not an appealing option. Oftentimes the clothes do not even fit correctly, and are just downright insulting.

* * *

Why should a disabled person be forced to sacrifice her dignity and grace for a pair of pants that is ugly yet functional while other able-bodied women indulge the opportunity to spend on cute designer jeans? In her TED Talk, Sinéad

Burke discusses the need for design to become more inclusive, by marrying form to function.[111] Think about it. If you are disabled, you may be hindered by an asymmetrical body or weak limbs. Burberry custom-designed a full wardrobe for Sinéad in preparation for her appearance in *The Business of Fashion* feature, *The Age of Influence*.[107] How crazy and awesome is that?

And Burberry is not the only brand that has taken it upon itself to customize clothes for the disabled community. Tommy Hilfiger released a collection for disabled adults following the brand's first collection back in 2016 for children. The goal, Hilfiger states, is "to democratize fashion."[112] The new, adaptive collection features adjustable garment length and magnetic closures for people with use of only one hand.

Other brands develop adaptable fashion for people with disabilities, like Adaptawear, which caters toward people with dexterity limitations.[113] Yet few mainstream designers have hopped aboard this inclusivity movement. Given the vast number of people living with disabilities, why has fashion still not wholeheartedly embraced the opportunity to expand their consumer base? I wonder if this is in part because different disabilities require different adaptations. There is no standard body type for people with disabilities, so clothing must be customized.

* * *

According to the US Department of Labor, disabled Americans have a purchasing power of $175 billion. That's a lot of money.[114] When we consider this fact, the question then becomes: why are all brands not jumping on this opportunity to attract new customers? Now this alone should indicate to fashion houses that there is a major market for creating fashion for people with disabilities. I can only hope that in the coming years we will begin to see more inclusive design that effortlessly combines functionality with aesthetic appeal. Disabled folks want stylish clothing options, too.

Accessible Fashion at Parsons Open Style Lab

Parsons Open Style Lab is making waves within the realm of accessible fashion. Originally founded in 2014 as a public service project by MIT, the Parsons Open Style Lab has since expanded to become a collaborative course for students to engage directly with the issues of dressing people of diverse abilities.[115]

Those at the Parsons Open Style Lab commit to creating technology-based wearables for people of all abilities. The industry refers to this as adaptive fashion. The sad reality is the fashion styles we see on runways are not made to be accessible for consumers of varying abilities. "We see [clothing] as an opportunity for greater accessibility and independence for quality of life," says Grace Jun, executive director of OSL and assistant professor at Parsons.[116] "But we also see a barrier to your independence if it takes you thirty minutes to put on a garment that has difficult closures because you have paralysis or limited dexterity in your fingers. Is it *really* your fault—or is it your clothing that needs to be redesigned?"

Good question. This is something I've thought a lot about over the past year-and-a-half as I struggle to learn ways to dress myself with ease. Initially following my stroke, I was completely paralyzed on the left side of my body and therefore unable to do simple tasks like put on a pair of pants, tie my shoes, or button my shirt. However, with some help from my incredibly determined and invested physical and occupational therapists, I learned some tricks to do these tasks on my own.

For example, I initially had to change all my shoelaces to elastic shoelaces so I didn't have to ask someone to tie my shoes every time I put them on. But one day a therapist told me that it was possible to tie my shoes with one hand, and taught me how to do it. I love learning cool little hacks like this for daily tasks. And now I'm practicing using my left hand, so hopefully I will be able to tie my shoes with both hands. But for now, the one-handed hack works.

Social initiatives like Parsons Open Style Lab push the

boundaries on adaptable fashion and redefine societal preconceived notions and ideas around disability. Sinéad Burke talks about the power of imagery in reshaping social conceptions.[107] And Sinéad's work in fashion activism is about so much more than raising awareness of the disabled community. In order for disabled populations to truly feel accepted by the fashion industry, they must have a seat at the table. "There needs to be power sharing," Sinéad says.[107] There must be disabled individuals in positions of power and influence to open up the minds of fashion executives.

Parsons Open Style Lab harnesses the power to engage with underrepresented audiences in exciting new ways, and thankfully it isn't the only modern incubator for adaptable fashion. Wolford, the luxury hosiery and swimwear boutique, upped its game by filing a patent on seamless technology, for "more comfort and functionality."[117] The trend on tech-infused wearables is an indicator to a larger macro-trend in digitalization.

Technology isn't going anywhere and will only continue to directly influence our lives. New advancements in technology for fashion, from the Apple watch to the ubiquitous chatbots on e-commerce sites, only scrape the surface of the absolute power and impact of tech companies. The more companies that turn to inclusive technological solutions for common dressing problems, the better equipped our society will be to handle the problems faced by consumers with disabilities.

On the Runway

With all the advancements being made in terms of diversity and inclusion in fashion, people are starting to take note of the racial diversity on the runways. In Marc Jacobs' Spring 2018 runway show, over half of the models were people of color.[118] Until now, the fall 2016 season had been the most racially diverse, with 31.9 percent nonwhite model castings.[118] The Fall 2017 season came close, featuring 31.5 percent non-white models.[118] Therefore, it was monumental for the industry to see such a rise in racial diversity.

The Fall 2017 season was the first time New York Fashion Week runways featured at least one model of color, and the spring season featured at least two models of color on every runway.[119] Fashion is clearly starting to listen to the need for diverse representation on the runway to appeal to a wider audience. A diversity report by The Fashion Spot emphasized improvements in the number of non-white, plus-size, and trans models walking the 2018 Spring shows.[119] I can't wait to see even more inclusivity on the runways in coming seasons.

You used to never see transgender models walking the runway, and now it is increasingly more common to see people like Australian Andreja Pejic, who became known around the world as the first fully androgynous supermodel, to walk runways and advocate for trans rights.[120] Pejic was first scouted as a model when she was seventeen and working at a McDonalds in Melbourne, Australia.[120] Pejic gained international recognition for modeling both men's and women's clothing. In the 2011 Paris fashion shows, Pejic walked for both the Marc Jacobs and Jean-Paul Gaultier shows, but concerns were expressed that her presentation as gender-fluid could be misconstrued for presenting as a topless woman.[120]

Vogue covered Andreja as the first openly transgender model.[121] She was the first transgender model to receive a major contract with beauty company Makeup Forever. [121]Andreja stated in an interview with *USA Today* that she hopes her experience can open up doors for other trans models. "It's amazing to show that I can be successful and that I can do what any other female model can do," she says.[122]

Andreja Pejic also serves as an activist for the trans community and aims to empower other women by sharing a message of positivity. A *Vogue* interview with Andreja states that, "she engages—and dismantles—all one's visceral perceptions of gender."[121] Pejic underwent gender confirmation surgery in 2014 and there has been no stopping her since. Pejic represents "a cultural and political mainstreaming of transgender identity" that has been long overdue.

"It is about showing that this is not just a gimmick," Pejic says. No other model has been able to successfully cross the line between traditionally male and female clothing quite like Andreja Pejic. "There are just more categories now," Pejic tells *Vogue*.[121] "It's good. We're finally figuring out that gender and sexuality are more complicated."[121] So what does this mean for the future of the fashion industry and trans models?

President of IMG Models, Ivan Bart, focuses on spreading a message of inclusivity and diversity to the industry.[123] IMG supports many models who lie on the periphery of traditional gender identity norms. They've championed fuller figured women like Ashley Graham and Candice Huffine, as well as wheelchair user Jillian Mercado.[123] Then, they made worldwide news with the announcement that they had signed Zach Miko, who became the world's first male plus size model.[123]

IMG's signing of Zach Miko expands the conversation around body positivity. Bart works to shift the conversation in fashion to increased diversity and more inclusive representation of all people. "We see it as an opportunity to change the conversation on diversity, inclusion...and this goes beyond size. It's about race, it's about age, it's about what we see the future as. Millennials have been living on a device since they were born, and one thing that's very positive about this generation is that they don't want to be fooled. They don't want to be sold. They want to know it's real. They don't buy into airbrushing, because they've been sending each other selfies since they were kids. And so they know what a picture really looks like, they know what their friends look like, so they don't want to look like this ultimate vision of perfection."[123] If millennials today seek a more authentic and real representation of people like them in fashion, the whole industry should be jumping at the opportunity to engage with a wider audience.

What to Watch For:

- Millennial push for more realistic and relatable faces in fashion
- Movement embracing size inclusivity
- Increased activism and raised awareness around the issues of those typically left out of the fashion conversation
- Brands like Tommy Hilfiger are starting to listen and design for consumers with disabilities. Adaptive design will only continue to become more relevant, as the number of disabled people increases. If we don't begin to create fashion that is more inclusive and available for people of all abilities, we will be leaving out a large portion of the population from the conversation.
- Increased integration of retail experience for adaptable fashion
- Consumer call to action addressing the needs of underrepresented groups and urging companies to pay attention to their unique needs
- Runways featuring more models of color
- Diversity of size and gender identity on the runway

PART 8

THE CHANGING FACE OF LEADERSHIP

"We are in a place right now where you have power as a talent," said Tina Tchen, a lawyer spearheading the Time's Up Legal Defense Fund and former chief of staff to First Lady Michelle Obama.[124] "We are in a tight labor market—if [businesses] want the best talent, they are coming to realize they need millennial women," she says.[124] Tchen spoke about dispelling stereotypes throughout her career as a corporate litigator. "You can see the look on a CEO's face when I walk in the door. An Asian woman is supposed to be quiet, demure, unassuming and here I come.... The thing I learned from that is not to get my anxiety up."[124]

A study conducted by *The Business of Fashion* revealed that the vast majority (73 percent) of fashion companies are led by white male chief executives.[125] The companies included in the survey were LVMH, Nike, Inditex, Dior, Kering, Hermès, TJX, Richemont, Adidas, Fast Retailing, Luxottica, Ross Stores, VF Corp, H&M, Swatch Group and Tapestry.[125]

On average, men and women of any ethnic minority represented only 11 percent of the board of directors at these companies.[126] Among US fashion companies, representation averaged 22 percent, seven points higher than American companies surveyed in a January 2018 McKinsey report.[119] In Europe, the average dropped to only six percent.[126] Of the largest 15 companies, six have no minority representation on their boards: Fast Retailing, H&M, Hermès, Inditex, Luxottica and LVMH.[126]

"The world is changing now and we need people to think differently in order to be successful," says Steve Baggi, leader of retail and consumer practices at London-based search and advisory firm, Green Park.[127] "Diversity is just one piece of that jigsaw puzzle."

A report by McKinsey showed that companies with more diverse employees are more likely to retain them.[128] Diverse teams are also better for tapping into diverse markets.

Harvard Business Review found in a survey of 1,700 companies that those with above-average diversity—in terms of gender, education, age and other factors—were more innovative, generating 19 percentage points more sales from products introduced in the last three years.[128]

Jen Rubio, cofounder of luggage brand Away, says the company's leadership needs to reflect the diversity of the brand's growing consumer base as it enters new markets.[129] Rubio herself represents part of that audience as a Filipino American immigrant.[129] The company's board is small, only four people, but three members are women and two represent ethnic minorities.[129]

Leadership behavior is increasingly important. Consumers care about the values of the leaders of the brands they shop from and want them to align with their own. The key to increasing leadership diversity first begins in recognizing that there is a problem. Companies need to realize what steps they can take to help more people achieve success.

Ethnically Ambiguous

Jessica Clark is a model who has benefited greatly from her ethnically ambiguous looks. She writes about her experience as a model, channeling her racially ambiguous features to her advantage to book modeling jobs.[130] With her curvy figure and dark hair, she fit right in during fashion's Brazilian obsession. Brazilian women would approach her, babbling off in rapid Portuguese, only for Clark to admit that she did not understand.[130]

Clark writes that there are not enough jobs for non-white models, and that "the limited number of available bookings also serves to limit agencies' interest in taking on non-Caucasian models."[130] She continues to write that now it is even more important than ever for stars who launch their own beauty lines and those in fashion to sell more than just a product.[130] Consumers want to see a product packaged and branded with a relatable message.

Know your Market

Diversity is a vague term. I've touched a bit on racial diversity in fashion to make the point that, while the industry is certainly improving by embracing people of varying backgrounds, there is still much work to be done. And not just racially.

"Them"

The past few years have been characterized by massive shifts in consumer behavior and preferences on a macro level. Consumers today feel the calling for a heightened sense of global togetherness and inclusion. And this extends far beyond racial diversity. We see an increased blurring of gender, evolving beauty standards, and inclusive design as prominent issues rising to the spotlight. Conde Nast's LGBTQ digital platform and media outlet, "Them," has received criticism for a name that unintentionally others vulnerable communities, drawing a clear distinction between "us" and "them."[131]

But even the rise of controversial platforms like "Them" reflect the broader global trend of authentic messaging and branding. Consumers today clearly have no problem with sacrificing brand loyalty in favor of a new company that better embraces their particular set of beliefs and values.

Melissa Moylan of Fashion Snoops touches on the idea of brand inclusion and knowing your customer base well. "As a brand you have to have tunnel vision because you have to know your customer," she says.[132] "In forecasting what I think is amazing and which keeps our eyes open is that we have such a diverse clientele and we're also global so we have to have our eyes peeled to all of that."[132]

Trend forecasters observe and take a note of everything from cultural shifts and tendencies to influential political agendas. Diversity is definitely a topic on fashion companies' minds now. "In culture we did a report recently that was on the plus-size market and how this is something a lot more brands need to be picking up on. It's not served very well right now, Moylan shares.[132] Everything from size inclusive options to inclusive beauty standards must be accounted for. If we don't bring these issues of improper representation to the forefront, they will never be effectively addressed.

Changes in Fashion Imagery

"It's time to try taking a risk for once," says Tyler Mitchell in his autobiographical short film for American Eagle in February 2017.[133] Tyler and I both attended high school in Atlanta, Georgia my freshman year. I only lived in Atlanta for one year, but have followed Tyler's already successful career as a photographer and filmmaker since relocating. Thanks to none other than the Queen B herself, Mitchell shot Beyoncé for the September issue cover of *Vogue.*[134]

At just 23 years old, Tyler Mitchell has become the first black photographer to shoot a *Vogue* cover.[134] Beyoncé has been known for supporting black artists, and agreed to pose for the cover under the condition that she have full creative control of the shoot. Using Tyler Mitchell as *Vogue's* photographer signals a massive departure from the norm for an industry that tends to rely on a few established artists.[134] But the industry backing Mitchell for the project shows that fashion is opening up its doors to welcome a wider array of artists with diverse backgrounds.

Tyler Mitchell is one of the young innovators changing society's ideas around fashion imagery. Nick Knight is another famed photographer who has spent his career redefining fashion through image-making.

Fashion imagery today is an outdated mode of communication, as the print magazine declines in cultural relevance in favor digital platforms. British photographer Nick Knight speaks on the future of fashion imagery. "I've always liked the idea of moving forward. I've never been comfortable with the idea of looking toward the past," says Knight in a *Business of Fashion* interview.[128]

As a famous fashion photographer, Knight was one of the first people at the turn of the century to claim that technology would revolutionize the fashion industry. He founded Showstyle.com, a digital platform that combines fashion imagery with the latest digital technology.[135] He was one of the first to claim that technology could seriously disrupt the industry. It is the future of fashion. Fashion is hurting with the decreased consumption of fashion and print due to the sexual abuse scandals that have plagued media outlets. "This is the beginning of a new era… I think we're still just seeing the tip of the iceberg," he says.[135]

And this fashion revolution surely changes how people engage with images. Nick Knight stated in a *Business of Fashion* podcast interview that consumers today have a romanticized idea that things were better before the internet.[135] As a successful fashion photographer, Nick Knight says that the landscape is changing, and that one of the most important things now is embracing fashion in motion.[135]

Young designers today don't need the press and the glossies. They just need social media and a few key celebrities or fashion influencers to promote their brand. To consumers, the old system feels outdated and wrong. Clothes need to be seen in motion because that is how they are in real life. Why are we stuck thinking that the best way to view fashion is the still image?

Today virtually anyone has access to runway images and the latest trends through social media and the internet. You just need a phone and an internet connection. Knight mentions that at the beginning of the new medium, almost 100 percent of the clients will ask for film because they know it is a currency to move forward.[135] The focus of fashion film has to be on the clothes, and not on creating a narrative.

The press and fashion magazines are becoming more and more irrelevant. They simply don't carry as much weight as tools like Instagram or Pinterest because consumers can view the same trends in the comfort and ease of their own devices. In an instant, consumers can access images that previously were only available to those who attended the fashion shows.

You no longer have to sit front row of New York Fashion Week to get the experience of a fashion show because the images will be posted on fashion websites or blogged about by fashion aficionados.

The launch of Instagram IGTV, the app's long-form vertical video platform, affords fashion companies the opportunity to broadcast video content to followers for a more immersive experience.[136] Protection does not appeal to the newest generation of Instagram consumers. Instead, today's Gen Z and millennial customers desire authenticity in social media content over curated perfection. Instagram's video platform serves as an outlet for brands to extend their reach beyond posts and IG Stories.[136]

While Nick Knight has spent a lot of time working on fashion imaging, his goal now is to turn the medium completely on its head, essentially catalyzing a major industry shift. Knight says that at the time he entered fashion photography, the industry was virtually unrecognizable. "Photography has killed itself off with its pretentiousness, its backward looking, unwillingness to evolve," Knight adds.[135] And this unwillingness to evolve is precisely what Knight aims to change.

"You have to make fashion entertainment," he says.[135] "It isn't enough to plug in cameras and say here you go. It's the difference between getting three thousand and three million viewers. The whole fashion schedule is evolving too…cycles and distribution are changing when a buyer in Hong Kong can see the catwalk and buy the clothes immediately…"[135] In my opinion, a good fashion film instills a sense of desire in the viewer. The fashion film should not boast or impose a narrative on the clothing. The narrative is imbued in the clothing and should speak for itself. The fashion film simply acts a medium for this message to be conveyed.

For Knight, the image is never about the technology that is used to make it. "You don't care what paintbrush a painter uses, and you shouldn't really care what technology a photographer or an image-maker uses. It's about what you're trying to say. It's about your appreciation, or your love, or your desire for what you've got in front of the camera," Knight elaborates.[135] In other words, you could have all the right tools and supplies to produce a truly great fashion film or still image, but without the creativity and talent on the end of both the photographer and the model, the product will remain uninspired.

What to Watch For:

- New innovations on social media channels like Instagram revolutionizing fashion imagery and how consumers engage with this content
- The push for a more inclusive social media experience to attract and retain the interest of new customers

- Products packaged and branded with a message to capture consumer interest
- Inclusivity encompassing more people from varied backgrounds in positions of power

PART 9

SHIFTING BEAUTY STANDARDS

As fashion focuses now on inclusivity of gender, race, ability, and size, it is also important to mention the increasing diversity of beauty standards.

Body Positivity

Maggie Rizer Mehran is an American supermodel whose "quirky" beauty has been featured on magazine covers around the world.[137] From covers on *Vogue* to *Harper's Bazaar*, Maggie has benefited from the industry's infatuation with pale skin, freckles, and red hair.

Maggie says that beauty standards in the fashion industry are always evolving. Sometimes beauty standards dip back into the past and then look forward to modernize.[137] She says her involvement in fashion has influenced and shaped her perception of beauty today.[137]

The fashion industry tends to promote unrealistic beauty standards for unattainable sizes. Maggie says that given the impractical beauty expectations perpetuated by the industry, it was refreshing to hear confirmation from the industry that beauty encompasses all ranges of looks. "Hearing the validation that health and beauty is important encourages you to lead a healthier lifestyle," Maggie tells me.[137] Hearing this validation served as a wakeup call for Maggie to prioritize her health and showed her that she could still be a successful model doing so.

Steps like regulating the age of models to ensure they are not too young and prioritizing health will change fashion for the better. Maggie understands the importance of health in beauty, and I can only hope this positive message continues to catch on with the rest of the industry.

Maggie also shared her gratitude in being appreciated for her individuality by the fashion industry.[137] Receiving validation from top designers like Donatella Versace and Miuccia Prada doesn't hurt, either.

Maggie's story of body positivity and health interests me because I face daily reminders of my limitations. Whenever I'm out, I constantly encounter people who stare at my leg as I'm walking by. I'm sure that (for the most part) it's not a conscious choice, but I still notice and dread the stares every time. Call me naïve or idealistic, but I dream of a world that truly embraces body positivity and no one stares. I dream of a world that is more accepting.

Changing Beauty Standards for Young Women—Self-Improvement

Especially within the last few years, beauty standards have intensified, and the bar has been raised for perfection through thoughtfully curated images. It is increasingly common for young twenty-something women to invest in anti-aging creams in an attempt to maintain their youth. Our need as young women to constantly self-surveil and improve personal hygiene and beauty can only be attributed to the beauty industry boom and the unrealistic standards beauty brands place on young women.

Amanda Hess wrote in The New York *Times* about a new "beauty-standard denialism": the "expectations for female appearances have never been higher," she writes, and yet it's "become taboo to admit that."[138] Beauty has become a form of self-empowerment for women, and yet we at times can get lost in keeping up with these standards imposed on us by the industry.

Women perceive improving their looks to be a mandatory process essential to health and complying with the status quo. FaceGym is a studio that claims to help women preserve their youthful beauty by following the mantra, "muscles first, skin second."[138] Exercise for the face is important too. And women of all ages, from mid-twenties to late sixties, tread the thin line between vanity and fitness in the hopes of maintaining youth.

While I don't necessarily condone the idea of Face Gym, I do see the appeal. Face Gym reminds me of the face exercises I have to do daily for my rehabilitation. After suffering a traumatic brain injury, I had a form of facial paralysis, or bell's palsy. It's a common side effect of a stroke. Nerve damage makes the facial muscles weak, causing them to droop. For months I couldn't get the left side of my face to show expression or smile, so it oftentimes looked like I was mad, when really I just couldn't move my face. In therapy I was given facial exercises to retrain the muscles—smiling, puckering, and speech exercises. With tons of practice my smile and vocal inflection improved, but I still have to make an active effort to smile evenly.

While I wasn't doing daily face exercises to preserve my youthful looks, if that's an unanticipated result, I'll take that, too.

And speaking of youthful preservation, the left side of my body should remain wrinkle-free. I've been receiving Botox injections on my left side every few months to help improve muscle tone. It's worked wonders with my rehab, and hopefully keeps away the wrinkles, too.

What to Watch for:

- Flourishing body positive movement to embrace people of all looks and sizes
- Shifting beauty standards to an appreciation for individuality

PART 10

FASHION AS EMPOWERMENT

"Rather than trying to change the world to «support girls, it's more efficient to support girls so they can change the world."

—MOLLY LOGAN

Brring! My alarm blares the time loudly: 6:15 a.m. I roll over to rest for five more minutes and then get up to begin my day. I pull off my blanket and undo the Velcro on my hand splint, which keeps my fingers straight and loose during the night so they don't tighten into a fist.

Once the splint is off, I shimmy out of bed to brush my teeth and wash my face. After my morning routine, I return to my bedroom and choose an outfit for the day. Today's clothing consists of a button down shirt, a pair of flare jeans, and my everyday sneakers. Here we go: left (weak) arm first, and then right. Once I have the shirt on, I grasp the fabric of the shirt steady with my left hand, and use my right to stabilize the other end and thread the buttons through the holes in the fabric.

* * *

No one would ever know unless they saw me getting dressed in the morning, but it took me months to learn how to button a shirt on my own. I feel so lucky that I have such dedicated therapists who are committed to helping me get better and learn new ways to accomplish the everyday tasks of independent living that I previously never gave a second thought.

It took me months to be able to use my left hand to assist in the process of buttoning a shirt, even if it is just loosely stabilizing fabric while my right hand does most of the work. Getting dressed in the morning, an activity that used to be second nature and is now a daily struggle, may seem to take me ages, but I just remind myself that a year ago this task would have been literally impossible.

The hard work I have invested in the tedious and repetitive tasks like buttoning a shirt or opening the refrigerator door, pays off in the increased ease with which I navigate these tasks.

It is so empowering for me to find new ways to tackle difficult activities and succeed! And who knows, come next year these activities may be even easier for me than they are now. With the right focus and determination, anything is possible!

Fashion is embracing today's cultural movement of empowerment through dress. Read on to learn how today's innovators use fashion as a tool to empower and inspire.

Halima Aden

"What a great time to be yourself. It's 2018, the year of female empowerment. It's the generation of uplifting other women. We are finally getting our voices heard, and it's not just one certain woman. It's all of us from different backgrounds, different walks of life. It's a great time to be a girl," says Halima Aden, the first model and activist to be featured in a hijab on the cover of British *Vogue*.[139] From her first foray into fashion in the Miss Minnesota USA beauty pageant, Aden has continuously challenged and redefined industry norms. Her modeling agency, IMG, agreed to her condition of conservative dress for fashion shoots and that she be allowed to wear her hijab.[139] Surprising that this had never been done before.

To Halima, fashion isn't about conforming to the latest trends or wearing something you're not comfortable with just to fit in. Girls shouldn't feel like they have to change who they are to be accepted by society. They should feel free to just be themselves. "I feel like it's my job to set the precedent for other girls, so that girls entering the industry shouldn't be afraid to ask for a private dressing area or a female stylist. I've already done it. It hasn't held me back. I dress differently from other girls, but if some skin is showing, I say, can we switch it? Doing it the right way, it's about who you are—it's not always about fitting in," Aden comments.[139]

Halima Aden sets a powerful precedent for other women to not just accept things as they are. Instead, girls need not be afraid to ask for what they want and make sure their needs are respected. Halima understands that representation matters. It is vitally important for girls to see people in the fashion industry who look like them and feel relatable.

Aden was born in a refugee camp in Kenya and migrated to the United States as a child.[139] She has made it her mission to empower other girls to pursue their dreams by redefining the realm of possibility. "We had women in the past in our community—doctors, lawyers, those amazing women we could celebrate and look up to. But we never really had somebody in fashion. So for young girls it's about having representation in mainstream media," Aden adds in an interview with British *Vogue*.[139] Aden wants to return to the refugee camp she grew up in and show the girls there is life outside the camps. "I want to say, 'I'm here! I've lived a day in your life, but I grew older and I grew wiser and now I'm doing this'. Not 'Now I'm a model!' but still, 'I left the country'. A dream beyond the border—kids don't see that."[139]

Halima Aden certainly inspires me to work hard at my goals and push beyond what I originally thought possible. A lot of hard work and the right attitude can take you a long way.

Girl empowerment at Voices 2017

What can fashion do to empower girls? This central question resounded at the 2017 Business of Fashion Voices conference. "Knowledge is power and it's empowering for young women," began model activist Karlie Kloss at the conference.[140] "It can change the way girls think about themselves and [what they think] they are capable of, but confidence is key. It's a tricky time, deciding who you think you can be and what you think you can't. [We need] more girls in the conversation, at the table," she says.[140] And fashion is listening to Kloss, who herself founded Kode with Klossy, a summer coding program for girls.[140]

Girls possess an arsenal of untapped creativity and innovation, but because of rampant gender inequalities around the globe, many girls do not get the chance to act on these desires. It's an issue of finding ways to harness the creative potential of girls by opening up doors and providing them with more opportunities to contribute.

Currently thirty-two million girls around the world should be in secondary school but aren't.[141] The Voices conference proved to be critical as it underscored the need for fashion to attract girls and show them there are opportunities.

* * *

Another question that arose in the BoF Voices conference was the issue of how to empower more girls to undertake initiatives in fashion. Kloss emphasized the importance of establishing support networks and communities that encourage learning to dispel the idea that "you can't."[140]

That being said, the fashion industry has a responsibility to use its voice and influence to positively impact girls around the world. "If every brand, retailer and content producer can see their day-to-day job through the lens of empowering women and girls, we will see a definitive wave of change," says Chris Anderson, cofounder of The Future Laboratory.[140]

One of the most important things to empower girls and show them the wide range of possibilities that exist is to create open dialogue between the fashion industry leaders and the broader community of girls. Sharing success stories of women who have "made it" in fashion opens girls' eyes to the endless realm of possibilities. Female empowerment is not just a fad or a passing trend. It is a cultural movement that will only continue to inspire women around the world.

Women @** Dior**

In 2017, French fashion house Christian Dior launched a mentorship program, Women @Dior, to empower young women interested in fashion.[142] The initiative coincided with International Women's Day, which provided a convenient platform for women's empowerment. Female students in Paris were invited to tour the Dior atelier and offices.[142] The idea is that by pairing young women with a Dior employee, they can have productive conversations to help launch their careers.

Tai Beauchamp

Women like Halima Aden have taken it upon themselves to inspire other women. Tai Beauchamp, an internationally recognized style influencer and entrepreneur, is no stranger to the challenges of empowering women in this day and age. Tai works to inspire women through fashion and style. Through her experience as fashion and beauty editor at top publications such as *Harper's Bazaar, Seventeen*, and *The Oprah Magazine*, Tai has helped women all over discover and appreciate their own inner and outer beauty.[143]

Tai founded Tai Life Media, a digital platform providing style inspiration and daily motivation for women.[143] The plethora of interviews and style content empowers women to live fully their best selves. She has experienced great success and fulfillment in a career that spans entrepreneurship, beauty, fashion and style. This journey has taken her from fashion and style to "living fully."[143] I was excited to hear more from this media maven about the connection between style and empowerment.

Tai articulated the importance of always working toward your impact and helping others by sharing your experiences. "It's important to figure out what your impact can and will be," Tai says.[143] "Impact is your opportunity to be in service to others and to yourself. What can others extract from my experiences? And then will I feel empowered and good at the end of what I'm doing?" she probes.[143]

Tai first realized the impact she was having on other women while working at *Seventeen*. The magazine was doing a cover of real girls to see if they could impact their lives by sending them to the dermatologist for the first time.[143]

One of the girls was rather unforgettable. After the month-long trial, she approached Tai to tell her that she had totally changed her life by sending her to the dermatologist to treat her acne.[143] To think that such a simple act would have such an impact on another person showed Tai that she was actually working toward something substantial and meaningful.

Her work in fashion editing and in her own company has been one huge lesson in how to deal with challenges. As she told me, "There will always be setbacks, but if you continue to persevere, and in my case stay faithful and grounded in your faith, you'll recover."[143] Truly inspiring words. Tai certainly empowers and motivates me to find my area of impact and home in on my specific strengths and skills. And do so fashionably, no less.

Leandra Medine, Man Repeller

Leandra Medine, founder of the ever-popular fashion blog Man Repeller, sites her convoluted dating history with the founding of the brand. At the time, Leandra was a junior in college and dating three guys on and off.[144] One day when she was in Topshop trying on clothes with a friend, her friend commented that she was not surprised that none of the men Leandra was seeing at the time I wanted to formalize their relationship with her because she "dressed like a psychopath." The way she dressed rendered her a man repeller.[144]

Leandra thought "Man Repeller" would be a great name for a blog, and so she went home, wrote up a definition, and launched her site. "I've always had a very unique relationship with fashion because for me it was always about self-expression and identity," she says.[144] "It takes me a minute to actually articulate what I'm feeling and clothes do that for me much quicker."

Her original definition for Man Repeller, "outfitting oneself in a sartorially defensive mode resulting in repelling members of the opposite sex," soon expanded beyond just an approach to fashion. "Why don't we make man repeller an attitude, a state of mind?" Leandra asked.[144] She decided to make it about female empowerment at a time when female empowerment was lacking. Her writing was "always veiled by a tinge of motivation," to show readers that man repelling can be a good thing, not to be taken literally.

Since Man Repeller's humble beginnings, Leandra Medine has managed to grow her brand while simultaneously empowering women to think highly of themselves and express their identity through personal style. She came to the realization of the importance of authenticity and self-empowerment when she was conducting research for her podcast, Monocycle, in which she interviewed the chief brand officer of Uber, Bozoma Saint John.[145]

Leandra was inspired by the way she spoke so highly of herself and trusted in her own ability to accomplish what she wanted. "How refreshing it was to hear a woman speak so highly of herself!" she thought. "How novel. How empowering."[145]

"As the decisions on my plate have become more important (and higher-stakes), I've learned that my noncommittal attitude toward decisiveness is a function of my lack of self-trust and the feeling that whatever decision I make is going to be the wrong one," she adds.[145] She goes on to say it has always been a struggle for her to accept her own words, and the past few years of her life have been spent seeking the validation of others instead of appreciating herself or the skills she has. Leandra Medine is ready to accept her self-worth and appreciate herself for who she is. She is just the example of self-acceptance American women need.

LoJo Bands

Female empowerment is certainly having a moment in fashion, and it is becoming even clearer through the start of more female-run businesses. Best friends Laura Fawzi and Julia Greenzaid have managed to build a successful online college apparel business.[146] I first met the two ladies our freshman year at Georgetown, and they wowed me with their creativity and determination in building their business. LoJo bands first began because the two girls share the passion for designing clothes.

They first began making changes to existing college apparel.[146] Think crop tops, cutouts, and their signature daisy ribbon embroidery. I was their first official customer back in freshman year when I ordered a Georgetown crop top with ribbon embellishments on the bottom. Since that first order, LoJo Bands has grown and expanded their repertoire to create stylish new takes on college apparel. "We look at on-trend brands and try to copy them with a college twist. Zippers and mesh design are very on-trend now, as is laceup design," the two tell me.[146]

Laura and Julia currently face all the challenges in starting and growing a business. "For all those little things we had no idea about (legal, taxes, copyrights, licenses) we had to hire people or get people to help us in forming the business and creating the LLC," they share.[146]

While creating the business has definitely not been without its fair share of challenges, Laura and Julia see a huge payoff in all of their work when they get to meet their customers at trunk shows. "People will tell us how much they love our stuff and how much they enjoy wearing it, and that's awesome," they say.[146] In fact, once a seven-year-old girl told Laura and Julia that she wanted to start a business when she's older just like them.[146] It's amazing how impactful these ladies are to other girls.

Gucci

Gucci CEO Marco Bizzarri told *The Business of Fashion* that he spends a lot of time talking to the people on the front lines of the company, from the seamstresses who make the product to the forecasters who discover the next trendy color scheme or fabric because he wants to show them he believes in their work.[147] The importance of positive company culture to empower employees cannot be understated.

Isn't this true in everyday life? In rehab, you are nothing if not positive. Other patients can lift you up, as well as the power of prayer.

One of my neighbors in rehab had been confined to a wheelchair for the past nine years. Anytime someone asked him how he was doing, a smile crossed his face and he'd respond, "Just chillin."

Marco Bizzarri believes in creating for lasting impact, as clothes produced just to keep up with trends will only last a few seasons.[147] Gucci has only just begun to scratch the surface of what is possible in terms of fashion as empowerment. By promoting and fostering a culture of creativity and by supporting all employees in their endeavors, Bizzarri demonstrates the changing culture of luxury and how it is even more important now to create related to passion.[147] By producing clothing that comes from a place of passion, Gucci won't be seen as one-season trendsetters, instead empowering consumers to pursue lasting style.[147]

What to Watch for:

- Consumer shift to interest in products created from passion instead of following trends
- Increasing representation in fashion and models like Halima Aden setting a powerful example for girls everywhere
- More women getting involved in fashion, using it as an outlet to share their creativity
- Boosting self-esteem for women through fashion is a major focus.

PART 11

BRAND PERSONALIZATION

Perhaps surprisingly so, one of the biggest struggles I face these days is pants shopping. Because I wear a leg brace, and I don't care too much to wear my brace over my pants, my options are seriously limited. Ultimately, I end up shopping exclusively for flared jeans that will cover my brace.

But if you've never done it before, you may be surprised to hear how difficult it is to actually *find* jeans that work with a brace. It took me months to find a couple of pairs that not only covered my brace, but that I was also able to successfully zip and button with one hand. (Pro tip: Abercrombie and 7 For All Mankind sell lots of flared jean options that stretch and aren't too difficult to button). *It's the small victories.*

* * *

No matter where you look or what you read about the future of retail, one thing is inevitably clear—brand survival heavily depends on companies' ability to successfully address the consumer desire for personalization. A study from the eMarketer Report shows that personalization is effective.[148] According to one study, 48 percent of US marketers reported that personalization on their websites or apps lifted revenues 10 percent.[148]

With all this talk about an impending retailpocalypse, brands are searching for new ways to engage with their customers and drive sales. I believe the future of retail and the secret to driving traffic to stores lies in a brand's ability to provide an authentic experience that feels personal. Customization is the key.

Piazza Sempione

I trundle through the Short Hills Mall in New Jersey toward a gathering of people and two cameras outside the Peloton boutique. I come to the mall often, typically early in the morning or in the evenings to practice walking. I feel so lucky that I'm even *able* to walk, so I don't like passing up any opportunity I get for movement. I never would have thought I'd see a day where I'm thrilled just to wake up in the morning and practice moving as much as I can, but I guess traumatic brain injuries have a funny way of putting things into perspective. That being said, on this particular morning I woke up with an extra boost of energy and determination to seize the day.

I had been looking forward to attending the Short Hills Mall spring and summer fashion trends presentation for a few weeks since I first heard about it. When you walk around the mall every day, you start to notice the smallest changes. While walking with my mom, we spied a poster for the spring and summer fashion trend show at the mall, and so we decided to check it out. The trend talk, presented by stylist and sustainable fashion entrepreneur, Gina La Morte, touched on everything from which shades of pink and coral to invest in for the coming seasons to the exciting navy and nautical themes that were sure to be a big hit in the summer months.[149]

I scanned the crowd and took a look at the clientele who had taken the thirty minutes out of their day to learn about the latest trends. And my jaw dropped. Sitting in front of me was a gorgeous woman in the most stunning and flattering A-line silhouette dress, paired with a chic pair of vintage Louis Vuitton heels. We approached her after the trend show to tell her that she looked gorgeous and inquire where she got her dress. "Oh this is from the boutique," she revealed.[150] "You should stop by, Piazza Sempione. We're right on the first floor by Tiffany's."

Later, walking through the mall, we decided to pop in the store and say hello. I was eager to speak with this stunning lady, and so I entered the store. Granted, I had passed by this boutique hundreds of times before but never once looked in to shop because I figured everything in there would be super expensive (and it was). I was expecting to walk into an intimidatingly vacant and exclusive shop, but I was only partly right.

The Piazza Sempione flagship boutique in The Short Hills Mall is the only one of its kind in the US. The company is headquartered in Italy, with locations in Rome, Milan, and New Jersey.[150] Walking into the Short Hills Mall location, I was overwhelmed immediately with the scent of luxury and exclusivity. I found the woman from the trend show, Karina Hoyos, and she immediately welcomed me in and showed me around the store.[150] I saw her gorgeous dress on the rack, available to purchase for a chill $1,200 (yeah, not happening).

Karina told me the key to the boutique's success lay in their personalization of the customer experience. Piazza Sempione prides itself on superior customer service.[150] Karina tells me that her customers love the exclusivity of a luxury brand that still relies on word of mouth to attract new customers.[150] Years ago when there used to be more boutiques around the country, customers would call in and ask if there were other locations. Piazza Sempione used to have boutiques in Chicago, Seattle, and Las Vegas, but has since consolidated to the one

Short Hills Mall flagship store.[150]

Many customers of that boutique were fans of the brand prior to the new location. And the Piazza Sempione boutique changed locations within the mall, which Karina tells me has helped increase foot traffic to the store. "For years, what has kept us strong without advertising has been the customer service," Karina tells me.[150] Customers visit the store expecting the full retail experience, which Piazza Sempione delivers.

This works to their advantage, as Karina says so many of the other high-end boutiques in the mall don't focus on customer service and experience as much. Karina says that in a sense, the Piazza Sempione team functions like therapists, listening and sharing in turn with clients. This makes the Piazza Sempione experience for the customer more personal. "As long as they feel comfortable with you, they will come back," Karina shares.[150]

And perhaps this little tidbit is the secret to creating and retaining brand loyalty. Piazza Sempione is a global company with customers from all around the world. Today's fashion consumer craves this holistic retail experience with an emphasis on great customer service. And at the end of the day, don't we all just want someone to talk with, someone we can share our life struggles and triumphs with?

Piazza Sempione homed in on this often-overlooked niche area of customer care, and made it their mission to show that they truly care about their customers and want to make them happy.

"We put outfits together depending on who the client is, her lifestyle, and the colors she likes. And we send it to them and they'll reply if they like it and we ship it out," Karina shares.[150] She hasn't even met a large portion of the shop's customers in person because they live all over the world. Customers expect the stylists at the store to know their wardrobe and their purchasing habits to be able to recommend wardrobe pairing options.

The Piazza Sempione signature is the Audrey trouser, named after fashion icon Audrey Hepburn.[150] Karina says customers will often share with the stylists their lifestyle and shopping habits in order to receive customized recommendations for their wardrobes. And her customers will tell her, "This is why I love coming here, because you remember. I love that you remember."

This extra thought and investment of stylists into not just their customers' clothing preferences but also in their lifestyle brings them back to the store each season. Piazza Sempione goes above and beyond to ensure quality customer service. Karina shares that her customers like to be called for special promotions in the store, and so she routinely makes calls each season to update her clients and offer them special promotions.[150] For their New York-based clients, Piazza Sempione will host events. For its most loyal customers, the boutique pairs with a New York-based PR firm to present a special Italian brunch with gifts for loyal customers.[150] The Piazza Sempione stylist speaks about the latest collection and its inspiration.

One of the main draws to Piazza Sempione is the brand's exclusivity and the fact that all clothing is made in Italy. Karina's main goal in the shop is to make her clients look and feel good. And more often than not, her customers will share with her their thanks. "You've spoiled me," they say. And they are spoiled with more than just a beautiful new dress or silk knit top, but by the thoughtful stylists in the shop who are more than willing to lend an ear and listen to them share their struggles. This personalization of brand experience sets Piazza Sempione apart from those that cater to the mass market.

An article in *The Business of Fashion* revealed that mass customization better aligns supply with demand, eliminating waste to make companies more sustainable.[151] Of the high-end luxury brands surveyed, only 21 percent offered any customization services.[151] Clearly the realm of personalization presents fashion brands with a tremendous growth opportunity to better align themselves with the consumer desire for customization.

Stitch Fix

Stitch Fix is a subscription-based, completely digitalized, personal shopping service.[152] Stitch Fix leverages data to deliver personalization on a mass scale. The business model is quite simple; Stitch Fix sends you clothing and accessories they think you will like, and you simply keep what you want and return what you don't. Stitch Fix's ability to deliver personalization at-scale differentiates them from other fashion and accessories brands struggling with finding ways to customize the consumer experience.[152]

Stitch Fix's CEO, Katrina Lake, spoke about her longtime interest in combining technology and retail, dating back to her undergraduate days at Stanford, in an interview with Harvard Business School.[152] She found it intriguing that brands still provided "fundamentally the same experience they had in the 1970s or even the 1950s despite how much the world has changed."[152] She wondered how brands might adapt and bring technology to retail in the twenty-first century. She wanted to be a part of the change movement.

Katrina Lake always loved data and knew it could be used to transform the retail experience. She embarked on a mission to create a new model for shopping. Stitch Fix combines data collection with the human element of serendipity in shopping. The brand collects data on its customers' tastes and physical measurements.[152]

She says that having a revenue that is dependent on style recommendations proves to be quite difficult. "Fit, style, material—these matter to all of us," she says.[152] And when you take into account the fact that everyone's preferences are wide-ranging and different, the whole process becomes more nuanced and difficult. The Stitch Fix team develops and utilizes algorithms to identify trends and prepare for stocking inventory more efficiently.

The example of Stitch Fix shows us just how much the industry has evolved in recent years. Personalization is the key to success in the retail world. Consumers increasingly seek brand experiences. Companies like Stitch Fix and Piazza Sempione continue to adjust to the changing fashion landscape and find innovative ways to engage with their consumers and offer them an experience beyond just buying a product. Stitch Fix and Piazza Sempione differ in their approach to engaging with customers; Stitch Fix uses a digital approach and Piazza Sempione relies primarily on word of mouth. Yet both brands fundamentally deliver personalized experiences to their customers, who can't wait to come back for more.

LAURA LEE

Laura Lee, founder of Laura Lee Designs, has made it her mission to embrace and promote individual style and creativity through her work. She designs accessories, from wallets and clutches to purses. "I was so tired of seeing so many women who were basing their status off of what they wore. To me it was really almost fad," Laura Lee tells me.[153]

An experience Laura Lee had once while in Shanghai totally altered her perception. Laura Lee tells me that while she was in Shanghai waiting for the metro, she was struck by the appearance of the woman standing next to her. They were almost dressed exactly alike, in the same Ralph Lauren suit, with Louis Vuitton bags and Tumi briefcases. "We looked like carbon copies of each other," Laura Lee admits.[153]

Fast forward six months later, and Laura Lee is in Bangkok. She tells me that while on the trip, she noticed a beautiful woman with no name-brand clothing. The experience impacted her so much that she was inspired to start her own unique accessories company, as nothing like it already existed on the market.[153]

After much hard work to get started and lots of running around to buyers, Laura Lee secured a position in a trunk show from a Henri Bendel buyer. The little voice inside her head told her: "If you don't do this, you're going to regret it."

"Anything that's impactful is worth the work," she told me.[153] Here was a great opportunity for her to make an impact in an industry she cared about. By addressing her own style challenges, the hope was that she could connect with and inspire other women who may be feeling the same sense of hopelessness.

Laura Lee has worked hard to build up her company, and it has achieved a level of success offering handmade products. "Each bag is different just like each woman is different. That's how we brand ourselves. No two bags are alike," she says.[153]

WONDERFUL WRAPS AND A LIFELONG LOVE FOR FASHION

Olivia Manduca understands from experience the necessity for product personalization. She had always been interested in fashion, even from a young age. When she was about seventeen, Olivia left her home in London to go live in the countryside. It was a hippie lifestyle, and Olivia spent her time living on her family's farm.[154] Finally free to live on her own, Olivia and her friends sought ways to generate income.

They began making crafts and selling them in the local town marketplace. However, this process was all very labor-intensive, and so Olivia and her friends searched for other means of making money.[154] She began collecting vintage beaded dresses, and acquired a great collection of forties and fifties dresses. Instead of making crafts, Olivia took her collection of vintage dresses to the marketplace and sold them for a small fortune.

Through this experience, Olivia realized that fashion was the business to be in. She continued to buy old clothing for resale and it was a success.[145]

Eventually she discovered what is today referred to as cabbage. London Fashion factories always have overrun stocks of clothes that they sell off privately or quietly, and so Olivia ended up buying the overstock and selling it for a vast profit.[154] She opened a shop and sold the cabbage. Olivia found designer shops in London that sold off their old clothing. She purchased it and sold her findings at the market.

"When I opened the shop I started making dresses but soon realized that was too labor-intensive," Olivia shares.[154] She left fashion in pursuit of the music industry, but ultimately returned to her passion for fashion.

Her love of fashion was reignited while she was preparing for her wedding. For the wedding Olivia wore a long cream dress, but struggled to find something to wear around her shoulders. "I looked everywhere and went to every designer," Olivia says.[154] "In the end a girlfriend said to me, I'll make one for you, and so we designed one in emerald velvet." It looked amazing, so Olivia proposed they start a business. "There was clearly a gap in the market, and people need shawls and drapes and wraps. There was nothing at the time," she adds.[154]

Olivia's friend handled the sewing while she went out and got different colored velvets and satins. Wonderful Wraps was originally intended to be a hobby, but the business took off and so the duo began to exhibit and do press articles. Olivia even exhibited next to Jenny Packham, the British designer known for her ready-to-wear runway couture.[154]

"The first place I tried to sell them was Harrods. I pulled strings to get an appointment, and they bought them. On the back of a big name, and as much press as I could get, I managed to sell to all the main high end shops around the world," Olivia says.[154]

While Olivia eventually sold Wonderful Wraps, the experience really opened her eyes to the importance of brand personalization. Wonderful Wraps ended up doing a lot of customized bridal shawls, one of which she gave to Princess Diana, who absolutely adored the deep purple drape.[154] Olivia's focus on giving customers the personalized wraps they desired ultimately contributed to the brand's success.

Lisa Gorlitsky Schafen

At the Fashion Footwear Association of New York, or FFANY, a tiny woman in an oversized tunic and heels struts down the runway.[155] The woman is a stark contrast from the 5'10" supermodels strutting down the runway just moments before. However, it is not the model's clothing that captivates the interest of the crowd, but rather, her shoe wear.

Lisa Gorlitsky Schafen may be best known for her acting career on shows like *Law & Order: Special Victims Unit*. However, her side career in shoe modeling interested me. Lisa said she began shoe modeling in her thirties, when a friend told her at a bridal party that her foot was perfect for shoe modeling. Lisa had no idea what a career in shoe modeling would entail, but she agreed to try it out. She went to an audition for Michael Kors, and the agent told her that her foot was a perfect size 6B. Not too wide and not too narrow.

"It's a crazy, strange job," Lisa says.[155] "What I loved about it is that it's sort of like being a fly on the wall. All these five-foot ten models and then there's little me on the table. It was a very interesting peek into a world that I otherwise would have had no part of. It was wonderful to sit back and watch this and be a part of the process. You learn very quickly that you have to have an opinion, that you have to speak up because they really need to hear how something fits. They like to know that I can give feedback straight from the prototype."[155]

The average shoe model is a size 6 B. The average runway model has a height between 5'8" and 5'10" and weighs 113 pounds, with a size 32 B bra.[156]

And now consider the average American woman, with a size eight and a half foot, height of 5-feet 4-inches, and definitely weighing more than 113 pounds.[157] The reality of the situation is that most Americans do not conform to fashion model standards. The majority of American women are shorter and heavier. Lisa happens to be lucky, because while she stands at just 5'2", her foot is the perfect size for the prototype. Designers can simply construct a shoe on her foot to fit. But in reality, most people don't have perfect size 6B feet, and require some form of adjustments.

This is why Lisa's work is a shoe model is so important. Without her feedback on shoe fit and functionality, designers wouldn't know how to create the shoe. Designers expect Lisa to give them feedback on how the shoe wears so they know what to change. In this sense, her shoe creation experience is personalized, and her perfect 6B shoe size sets the sizing standard.

During FFANY, Lisa spends her time in the showroom, trying on more than three hundred shoes for buyers. If only one company wants the shoe, designers ask the company if they want an exclusive. Otherwise they can't make the shoe. It could be a month-long process deciding who will buy what shoe and how many to make. Models test the sale samples, which can be uncomfortable because they're not approved for fit yet.[155] Companies will come in to look and make their best guess at what they think will pique customer interest. "They design with different customers in mind, and we also fit with different customers in mind," Lisa shares.[155]

Lisa works directly with designers on all kinds of shoes, acting as the consumer with the perfect fit.

Once the shoe prototype has been made, Lisa participates in fitting. She tells me that she's had to model and fit many unusual and ugly shoes. One brand, Life Stride, attempted to rebrand as a sexy, youthful label.[155] It didn't work.

One time at a Michael Kors show, Lisa was unexpectedly pushed into the runway rotation.[155] The buyers wanted to see shoes as well as clothes. After the last model finished walking down the runway, Lisa was stripped down, dressed in a tunic, and sent down the runway. It was such a shock to see a tiny 5'2" woman shoe modeling on the Michael Kors runway.

Lisa's experience sheds light on how shoes are created and customized. While all the shoes she models are constructed specifically to fit her perfectly sized foot, the reality is that most people's feet will not fit into the sample size. And this is where the need for personalization comes in. Perhaps brands can't just survive by making a set number of different sized shoes. The truth is people have different sized feet, varying arches, and widths. Brands' ability to adapt to the varying shoe needs of consumers proves to be the competitive edge in what is an old-fashioned industry still deeply rooted in traditional shoe-making standards and practices.

Customization: Smathers and Branson

The retail landscape is changing. It's no longer enough for brands to attract consumers through promotions and targeted ads. Consumers want a fully integrated retail experience and authentic brand interactions.

Terry Lundgren, executive chairman for Macy's, tells *Forbes* that the future of retail lies in customization.[158] "The whole concept of personalization is simply on steroids right now. It's all about the consumer in that one moment in time. We're doing anything we can do to connect directly with consumers and make shopping convenient for them," she says.[158] With the continued rise of mass-market fashion brands, consumers are expressing interest in a return to personalized products. The brands that will survive the supposed retailpocalypse will effectively iterate on this consumer desire for personalization.

* * *

Peter Carter and Austin Branson, founders of needlepoint accessories company Smathers and Branson, understand the importance of personalization in retail. The two friends started the company in 2004 after graduating college, and Smathers and Branson has only continued to grow since.[159] The brand's strong focus on customization sets them apart.

But the company wasn't always so intent on cultivating a brand experience based on customization. Whereas initially the two founders cared about creating hand-stitched needlepoint products en masse, when they started receiving tons of consumer requests for personalized Smathers and Branson products, the necessary company pivot became obvious.

And since the founders realized their brand's potential for expansion with a business model based on customized products, there has been no slowing down their growth. Part of the founders' success is due to their ability to execute on ideas. "Not all our products have been as wildly successful as we'd like, but we've been able to pivot and focus on what's working," says Peter Carter.[159] And personalization has proven to be the key driver of growth for Smathers and Branson.

Peter Carter shares that the beauty of the brand lies in its "ability to create something 100 percent unique."[159] Every

Smathers and Branson belt is specifically handmade by a single artisan, so each product is slightly different.[159] Because their custom and monogrammed products were well-received, Austin and Peter felt their business was ready to support a heightened level of customization.

Smathers and Branson offers everything from monogrammed wallets and key fobs to custom life belts to commemorate major events like weddings or graduations.[160] Smathers and Branson effectively capitalizes on their customers' desire for personalized products. I think in the coming years we will only continue to see success from brands that cater to consumers' desire for customized products.

What to Watch For:

- Customization of brand experience transforming consumer expectations and raising the bar for brand experience integration
- The importance of strong customer service in brand success
- More brands embracing personalization to appeal to younger consumers

EPILOGUE

"And stop," my therapist Todd says just as the timer rings. "Great work today. You beat your goal. You walked 1,501 feet in six minutes, over 100 feet further than when we did this test a few weeks ago. Now that's a record."

* * *

July 24, 2018, marked my one year anniversary of outpatient therapy. Over that year, I only missed a handful of appointments, meaning I have been coming biweekly to therapy for a year. I can't help but think how incredibly far I have come in this past year. I feel like I've accomplished more in this past year than I have in the twenty-two other years of my life.

While it may sound bizarre considering how difficult and

frustrating the past year was, I really do feel grateful for everything I've managed to accomplish. I learned to walk and move my arm, so that now I can focus on the finer motor skills like grasping with my hand and flexing my ankle. I always thought of myself as motivated and goal-oriented, but the experience this past year has elevated that to a whole new level.

I've learned so much, not just about how to use my leg and arm again, but more importantly about the importance having a strong support network of family, friends, mentors, and therapists who push me to better myself physically, emotionally, and spiritually. Every moment of the day I think how blessed I am that I get to wake up every morning and work toward my goals. I just as easily could have not survived the night of May 30th to be here today and share my story. But I did, and I wrote this book documenting my journey.

I hope this book sheds light on the cultural trends influencing fashion for my readers, and I hope you learned something. I understand now how fragile life is and I realize that each day is quite literally a blessing, so I must make the most of each day that I'm given. Thanks again to all those who have helped me along in this journey of recovery and self-discovery. In my wildest dreams I never would have thought I'd be capable of publishing a book, especially considering my recent life events. But processes like these open doors, and I'm so thankful for all the cool people I've had the chance to meet and talk with while writing this book. Life is awesome, and by taking it day by day, I can't wait to see what adventures are next in store.

And who knows, maybe this time next year I'll be wearing heels and zipping my jackets on my own. Anything's possible.

Maddi Niebanck

APPENDIX

[1] Zumbach, Lauren. "Beauty companies ramp up the pace to keep up with faster trends." Chicagotribune.com, 21 Feb. 2017, http://www.chicagotribune.com/business/ct-ulta-fast-beauty-makeup-trends-0221-biz-20170217-story.html

[2] Milnes, Hilary. "Speed-to-market: How luxury brands are picking up the pace of production cycles." Digiday.com, 8 Jan. 2018,

https://digiday.com/marketing/speed-market-luxury-brands-picking-pace-production-cycles/

Introduction

[3] The Business of Fashion and McKinsey & Company. *The State of*

Fashion 2018. McKinsey.com, 2017. https://cdn.businessoffashion.com/reports/The_State_of_Fashion_2018_v2.pdf

Sustainable fashion

[4] The Business of Fashion and McKinsey & Company. *The State of Fashion 2018*. McKinsey.com, 2017. https://cdn.businessoffashion.com/reports/The_State_of_Fashion_2018_v2.pdf

Part 1: Sustainability

What is sustainability?

[5] Hahn-Petersen, Luna Atamian. Businessoffashion.com. "Millennials say they care about sustainability. So, why don't they shop this way?" 21 Apr. 2018.

https://www.businessoffashion.com/articles/opinion/op-ed-millennials-say-they-care-about-sustainability-so-why-dont-they-dont-shop-this-way[6] LIM College. *LIM College Study Reveals That When it Comes to Buying, Millennials Are Not Eco-Fashionistas. Prnewswire.com.* 13 Feb. 2018.

https://www.prnewswire.com/news-releases/lim-college-study-reveals-that-when-it-comes-to-buying-millennials-are-not-eco-fashionistas-300597990.html

Millennials and Sustainability

[7] The Week staff. "5 Eco-friendly fashion choices." Theweek.com. 5 May 2018. http://theweek.com/articles/771308/5-ecofriendly-fashion-choices

[8] LaMorte, Gina. Personal interview. 27 Jun 2018.

[9] Slow Factory, slowfactory.com/.

[10] Hahn-Petersen, Luna Atamian. Businessoffashion.com. "Millennials say they care about sustainability. So, why don't they shop this way?" 21 Apr. 2018.

https://www.businessoffashion.com/articles/opinion/op-ed-millennials-say-they-care-about-sustainability-so-why-dont-they-dont-shop-this-way[11] Oeko-tex.com. "The Key To Confidence: What Does It Take To Build Trust with Busy, Sustainability-Minded Consumers?" 3 May 2018. Hahn-Petersen, Luna Atamian. Businessoffashion.com. "Millennials say they care about sustainability. So, why don't they shop this way?" 21 Apr. 2018.

https://www.businessoffashion.com/articles/opinion/op-ed-millennials-say-they-care-about-sustainability-so-why-dont-they-dont-shop-this-way[12] Blanks, Tim. "For Natalie Massenet, Change Brings Opportunity." Businessoffashion.

com. 16 Feb. 2018. https://www.businessoffashion.com/articles/bof-exclusive/for-natalie-massenet-change-brings-opportunity

Natalie Massenet

[13] De Klerk, Amy. "Natalie Massenet has launched a venture capitalist firm." Harpersbazaar.com. 17 Apr. 2018. https://www.harpersbazaar.com/uk/fashion/fashion-news/a19836129/natalie-massenet-venture-capital-firm-imaginary/

[14] Remy, Nathalie, Speelman, Eveline, Swartz, Steven. "Style that's sustainable: A new fast-fashion formula." Mckinsey.com. Oct. 2016. https://www.mckinsey.com/business-functions/sustainability-and-resource-productivity/our-insights/style-thats-sustainable-a-new-fast-fashion-formula

Reformation

[15] Chaykowski, Kathleen. "This Model Turned CEO Is Betting 'Bricks And Clicks' Can Create A Green Fast-Fashion Empire." Forbes.com. 24 Oct. 2017.

https://www.forbes.com/sites/kathleenchaykowski/2017/10/03/this-model-turned-ceo-is-betting-bricks-and-clicks-will-make-reformation-a-green-fashion-empire/#f9c319e27912[16] Lopez, Erica. "Yael Aflalo Is Building an Eco-friendly Fast Fashion Empire, and it Looks So Good." Nordstrom.com. 4 Jun 2018.

https://blogs.nordstrom.com/fashion/yael-aflalo-is-building-an-eco-friendly-fast-fashion-empire/https://www.forbes.com/sites/kathleenchaykowski/2017/10/03/this-model-turned-ceo-is-betting-bricks-and-clicks-will-make-reformation-a-green-fashion-empire/#f9c319e27912

[17] Bauck, Whitney. "How T-Shirt Brand For Days is Using a Membership Model to Minimize Waste." fashionista.com. 31 May 2018. https://fashionista.com/2018/05/for-days-sustainable-t-shirt-subscription

[18] "Full transcript: Jennifer Hyman, CEO of Rent the Runway, is creating the Spotify of women's clothes." recode.net. 9 Feb 2017. https://www.recode.net/2017/2/9/14566938/full-transcript-jennifer-hyman-ceo-rent-the-runway-subscription-womens-clothes

Elizabeth St. John

[19] St. John, Elizabeth. Personal interview. 10 May 2018.

[19] MarketLine. "Five Years since Rana Plaza, fast fashion demand still fuels unethical practices." Retail-insight-network.com. 26 Apr 2018. https://www.retail-insight-network.com/comment/five-years-since-rana-plaza-fast-fashion-demand-still-fuels-unethical-practices/

The Power of Celebrity

[20] Farra, Emily. "The Year in Sustainable Fashion Got Sexy - Read the Highlights Here." vogue.com. 7 Dec 2017. https://www.vogue.com/article/year-in-review-sustainability-stella-mccartney-gucci-tom-ford

[21] Spagnoli Gabardi, Chiara. "WTF IS PVC? WHY PVC CLOTHING IS A REALLY, REALLY BAD IDEA." eluxemagazine.com. https://eluxemagazine.com/magazine/pvc-clothing/

[22] Thomas, Dana. "Why Won't We Learn from the Survivors of the Rana Plaza Disaster?" nytimes.com. 24 Apr 2018. https://www.nytimes.com/2018/04/24/style/survivors-of-rana-plaza-disaster.html

[23] Murray-Ragg, Nadia. "Emma Watson Wears Vegan Fashion by Stella McCartney on Front Cover of *Vogue."* livekindly.co. 28 Feb 2018. https://www.livekindly.co/emma-watson-wears-vegan-fashion-on-front-cover-of-vogue/

Threats of fast fashion on the circular economy

[24] "A New Textiles Economy: Redesigning fashion's future." Ellenmacarthurfoundation.org. 28 Nov 2017. https://www.ellenmacarthurfoundation.org/publications/a-new-textiles-economy-redesigning-fashions-future

[25] "2020 Circular Fashion System Commitment." globalfashionagenda.com. http://www.globalfashionagenda.com/commitment/

[26] Malik Chua, Jasmin. "Circularity: Sustainable Fashion's Holy Grail or Greenwashing?" businessoffashion.com. 12 Jun 2018.

https://www.businessoffashion.com/articles/professional/circular-economy-the-holy-grail-of-sustainable-fashion[27] Gould, Hannah. "Zara and H&M back in-store recycling to tackle throwaway culture." Theguardian.com. 26 May 2017. https://www.theguardian.com/sustainable-business/2017/may/26/zara-hm-step-up-instore-recycling-tackle-throwaway-culture

[28] Goldberg, Eleanor. "You're Probably Going to Throw Away 81 Pounds of Clothing This Year." huffingtonpost.com. 9 Jun 2016. https://www.huffingtonpost.com/entry/youre-likely-going-to-throw-away-81-pounds-of-clothing-this-year_us_57572bc8e4b08f74f6c069d3

Gucci's explosive growth strategy

[29] Danziger, Pamela. "Gucci's Cracked The Luxury Code With Millennials,

Thanks To Its Dream Team of Bizzarri and Michele." Forbes.com. 16 Nov 2017. https://www.forbes.com/sites/pamdanziger/2017/11/16/

guccis-cracked-the-luxury-code-with-millennials-thanks-to-its-dream-team-of-bizzarri-and-michele/#1209fa831523

[30] Williams, Laura Lee. Personal interview. 13 Feb 2018.

Sustainability as Explosive Growth Strategy

[31] "The BoF Podcast: Inside Gucci's Explosive Growth Strategy" from The Business of Fashion. 23 Mar 2018. https://www.businessoffashion.com/articles/podcasts/the-bof-podcast-inside-guccis-explosive-growth-strategy

Part 2: Technology

AI chatbots and the rise of the see-now-buy-now model

[32] Johnson, Lauren. "5 Bleeding-Edge Brands That are Infusing Retail with Artificial Intelligence." adweek.com. 2Jan 2017. https://www.adweek.com/digital/5-bleeding-edge-brands-are-infusing-retail-artificial-intelligence-175312/

[33] Biron, Bethany. "Burberry launches 'see-now-buy-now' chatbot." Digiday.com. 16 Sept 2016. https://digiday.com/marketing/burberry-launches-see-now-buy-now-chatbot/

[34] Quoc, Michael. "Ecommerce brands succeeding with chatbots."

Abetterlemonadestand.com. 23 Oct 2017. https://www.abetter-lemonadestand.com/ecommerce-chatbots/

[35] White, Sarah. "Fashion firms dither over instant shopping on the catwalk." Reuters.com. 20 Feb 2018. https://www.reuters.com/article/us-fashion-retail/fashion-firms-dither-over-instant-shopping-on-the-catwalk-idUSKCN1G40RY

[36] Bennett, Farai. "Selena Gomez is the Highest Paid Celebrity on Instagram." businessinsider.com. 30 Jun 2017. https://www.businessinsider.com/selena-gomez-highest-paid-celebrities-instagram-2017-6

[37] Odell, Amy. "Are Influencers Really Worth the Money?" *The Business of Fashion*. 5 Jul 2018. https://www.businessoffashion.com/articles/professional/are-influencers-really-worth-the-money

[38] Del Ray, Jason. "Amazon won a patent for an on-demand clothing manufacturing warehouse." Recode.net. 18 Apr 2017. https://www.recode.net/2017/4/18/15338984/amazon-on-demand-clothing-apparel-manufacturing-patent-warehouse-3d

[39] Sawers, Paul. "Google and Zalando launch Project Muze, a machine-learning experiment for 3D fashion design." Venturebeat.com. 2 Sept 2016.

https://venturebeat.com/2016/09/02/google-and-zalando-launch-project-muze-a-machine-learning-experiment-for-3d-fashion-design/

Wearable tech:

[40] Lamkin, Paul. "Wearable Tech Market To Double By 2021." Forbes.com. 22 Jun 2017.

https://www.forbes.com/sites/paullamkin/2017/06/22/wearable-tech-market-to-double-by-2021/#63991bd9d8f3[41] Shirer, Michael. "IDC Forecasts Shipments of Wearable Devices to Nearly Double by 2021 as Smart Watches and New Product Categories Gain Traction." Idc.com. 20 Dec 2017.

https://www.idc.com/getdoc.jsp?containerId=prUS43408517

3D Printing

[42] Plate, Kristen. *Printed to the Nines: Why 3D-Printing Will Transform the Fashion Industry.* New Degree Press. 2017.

Biofabricated leathers

[43] ModernMeadow Press. Biofabricated leathers. Message to Maureen Ball. 13 Jun 2018. Email.

[44] "Zoa." ModernMeadow. http://zoa.is/

Part 3: Solidarity for a cause: Authentic brand messaging

[45] Zierer, Manuel. "Nike Supports the LGBTQ Community with its New BETRUE Collection." keller-sports.com. 9 Jun 2017. https://www.keller-sports.com/guide/nike-supports-the-lgbtq-community-with-its-new-betrue-collection/

[46] Ames, Eden. "Millennial Demand for Corporate Social Responsibility Drives Change in Brand Strategies." Marketing Health Services. https://www.ama.org/publications/MarketingNews/Pages/millennial-demand-for-social-responsibility-changes-brand-strategies.aspx

[47] "Kendall Jenner 'feels bad' after Pepsi Black Lives Matter advert controversy." Bbc.co. 2 Oct 2017. http://www.bbc.co.uk/newsbeat/article/41465222/kendall-jenner-feels-bad-after-pepsi-black-lives-matter-advert-controversy

[48] Chen, Cathaleen. "Fashion Got Woke. But at What Cost?" *The Business of Fashion. 30 May, 2018. https://outline.com/zmYWxy*

Political engagement and value system alignment

[49] "The BoF Podcast: Inside Gucci's Explosive Growth Strategy" from The Business of Fashion. 23 Mar 2018. https://www.businessoffashion.com/articles/podcasts/the-bof-podcast-inside-guccis-explosive-growth-strategy

[50] Chen, Cathaleen. "Fashion Got Woke. But at What Cost?" *The Business of Fashion. 30 May, 2018. https://outline.com/zmYWxy*

Fashion to Address Social Problems

[51] Givhan, Robin. "To fight the status quo, the activists of 1968 harnessed the power of fashion." *Washington Post.* 23 May 2018. https://www.washingtonpost.com/lifestyle/style/to-fight-the-status-quo-the-activists-of-1968-harnessed-the-power-of-fashion/2018/05/23/1d2f2ad2-44dd-11e8-bba2-0976a82b05a2_story.html?utm_term=.2dd58e4b828f

[52] Hodge, Kyle. "Kerby Jean-Raymond Shares the Story Behind Pyer Moss's 'American Also' Collection." highsnobiety.com. 8 Feb 2018. https://www.highsnobiety.com/p/pyer-moss-american-also-interview-video/

[53] Givhan, Robin. Personal interview. 21 Feb 2018.

[41] Odell, Amy. 5 Jul 2018. "Are Influencers Really Worth the Money?" businessoffashion.com. 5 Jul 2018.

https://www.businessoffashion.com/articles/professional/are-influencers-really-worth-the-money

Politics and Fashion

[54] Wolf, Cam. "New Balance, Under Armour, and the Year that Sneakers Got Political." *GQ*. 22 Dec 2017. https://www.gq.com/story/new-balance-sneakers-politics-2017

[55] Phillips, Michael. "The Elite Roots of Richard Spencer's Racism." Jacobinmag.com. 29 Dec 2016.

https://www.jacobinmag.com/2016/12/richard-spencer-alt-right-dallas-texas/[56] Givhan, Robin. "Neo-Nazis are using fashion in an attempt to normalize. The fashion industry needs to speak up."washingtonpost.com. 22 Aug 2017. https://www.washingtonpost.com/news/arts-and-entertainment/wp/2017/08/22/neo-nazis-are-using-fashion-in-an-attempt-to-normalize-the-fashion-industry-needs-to-speak-up/?noredirect=on&utm_term=.ae9f53abf6c6

Fashion as Protest: VSTRO

[57] Zorka, Zoe. "Activism through Fashion: How VSTRO is Fighting Inequality in the Most Fashionable Way." Thesource.com. 8 Feb 2018. http://thesource.com/2018/02/08/activism-through-fashion-how-vstro-is-fighting-inequality-in-the-most-fashionable-way/

Protest Messaging:

[58] Picquot, Heather. Personal interview. 23 Mar 2018.

[59] Arad, Itay. Personal interview. 17 May 2018.

[60] Ault, Nicole. "How much does culture matter in branding?" retaildive.com. 17 Jul 2018. https://www.retaildive.com/news/how-much-does-culture-matter-in-branding/527780/

[61] Yohn, Denise Lee.(2018) Fusion: How Integrating Brand and Culture Powers the World's Greatest Companies. Nicholas Brealey Publishing.

[62] Wang, Ucilia. "Patagonia pulls out of Utah trade show in protest of state's public land grab." Theguardian.com. 7 Feb 2017. https://www.theguardian.com/sustainable-business/2017/feb/07/patagonia-bears-ears-public-land-congress

[63] Women's ASOS Made in Kenya. http://www.asos.com/women/a-to-z-of-brands/asos-made-in-kenya/cat/?cid=25655

Building your tribe

[64] De Lisle, Vanessa. Personal interview. 7 Feb 2018.

[65] Batdorf, Alex. Personal interview. 26 Jan 2018.

Part 4: Young Innovators: the Importance of fostering community

Brand Promotion

[66] Hart, Jake. Personal interview. 26 Jan 2018.

Creating community

[67] Fernandez, Chantal. "SoulCycle Scales Community." *The Business of Fashion*. 1 Dec 2017. https://www.businessoffashion.com/articles/voices/how-soulcycle-scales-community

Spreading a positive brand message to community

[68] Cha, Kevin. "Introducing MADHAPPY." Nousculture.com. 2017. http://nousculture.com/madhappy/

[69] Sitt, Joshua. Personal interview. 24 Jan 2018.

Paolo Moreno, Antidote X

[70] Moreno, Paolo. Personal interview. 6 Feb 2018.

[71] "The Enormous Influence of Online Reviews." *The Week*. 2 May 2018.

http://theweek.com/articles/770712/enormous-influence-online-reviews[72] Bloem, Craig. "84 Percent of People Trust Online Reviews As Much as Friends. Here's how to Manage What They

See." Inc.com. 31 Jul 2017. http://theweek.com/articles/770712/enormous-influence-online-review

Part 5: Past Influence on new trends

[73] Sadick, Sydney. "Jamie Mizrahi on her first collection for Juicy Couture." Fashionweekdaily.com. 18 Dec 2017. https://fashionweekdaily.com/jamie-mizrahi-on-her-first-collection-for-juicy-couture/

[74] Farra, Emily. "2018 Ready-to-wear Juicy Couture." Vogue.com. 8 Feb 2018. https://www.vogue.com/fashion-shows/fall-2018-ready-to-wear/juicy-couture

[75] Syme, Rachel. "The Fate of the Juicy Couture Tracksuit in the Age of Athleisure." Newyorker.com. 28 Mar 2018. https://www.newyorker.com/culture/on-and-off-the-avenue/the-legacy-and-the-futureof-the-juicy-couture-tracksuit

[76] Petrarca, Emilia. "Paris Hilton's Most Iconic 2000s Looks, from Juicy Couture to Rhinestones." Wmagazine.com. 10 May 2017. https://www.wmagazine.com/gallery/paris-hilton-best-2000s-style/all

[77] Cheng, Andrea. "What do the Juicy Couture Founders Think of the Brand's Revival?" observer.com. 10 Oct 2017. http://observer.

com/2017/10/juicy-couture-founders-pamela-skaist-levy-and-gela-nash-taylor-on-the-brands-revival/

[78] "Pretty in pink! Elle Fanning stands out in eye-catching fuscia sweatsuit as she arrives at LAX." dailymail.co.uk. 12 Mar 2018. http://www.dailymail.co.uk/tvshowbiz/article-5489541/Elle-Fanning-stands-fuchsia-sweatsuit-arrives-LAX.html

Fashion Snoops trend analysis

[79] Picquot, Heather. Personal interview. 23 Mar 2018.

[80] "Kenzo Presents Britney Spears." kenzo.com. https://www.kenzo.com/us/en/kenzolovesbritney

Part 6: Diversity

[81] Bartley, Savon. Fashion Snoops Trend Immersion Day. 8 May 2018.

[82] La Ferla, Ruth. "The Glamorous Grandmas of Instagram." Nytimes.com. 20 Jun 2018. https://www.nytimes.com/2018/06/20/style/instagram-grandmas.html

The future of luxury and need for increased industry diversity

[83] Friedman, Vanessa and Paton, Elizabeth. "Louis Vuitton Names Virgil Abloh as New Men's Wear Designer." nytimes.com. 26 Mar 2018. https://www.nytimes.com/2018/03/26/business/louis-vuitton-virgil-abloh.html

[84] Stanley, Jack. "Here's What Fashion Insiders Think of Virgil Abloh at Louis Vuitton." hypebeast.com. 27 Mar 2018. https://hypebeast.com/2018/3/virgil-abloh-louis-vuitton-fashion-insiders

[85] Solway, Diane. "Virgil Abloh and his Army of Disruptors: How he became the king of social media superinfluencers." wmagazine.com. 20 Apr 2017. https://www.wmagazine.com/story/virgil-abloh-off-white-kanye-west-raf-simons

[86] "Virgil Abloh Named Louis Vuitton's Menswear Designer." usnews.com. 26 Mar 2018. https://www.usnews.com/news/business/articles/2018-03-26/virgil-abloh-named-louis-vuittons-mens-wear-designer

Rise of luxury streetwear

[87] A$AP Rocky. "Raf Simons." *Time.* 20 Apr 2017. http://time.com/collection-post/4736290/raf-simons/

[88] Morency, Christopher. "Why Rappers are Fashion's New Royalty." *The Business of Fashion. 21 May, 2018.* https://www.

businessoffashion.com/articles/intelligence/the-new-kings-and-queens-of-fashion-kanye-west-asap-rocky-cardi-b

[89] Morency, Christopher. "Streetwear Reigns Supreme, Say Teens." *The Business of Fashion*. 10 Apr 2018. https://www.businessoffashion.com/articles/news-bites/streetwear-reigns-supreme-say-teens-adidas-gucci

[90] A$AP Mob. Lyrics to "Raf." 2017. https://genius.com/A-ap-mob-raf-lyrics

[91] O, Allen. "Kanye West Performs in Celine 2011 Spring Silk Shirt at Coachella Festival." upscalehype.com. 18 Apr 2011. http://www.upscalehype.com/2011/04/kanye-west-performs-in-celine-spring-2011-silk-shirt-at-coachella-festival/

[92] Solomon, Michael. "How Millennials Will ReShape the Luxury Market." forbes.com. 20 Jun 2017.

https://www.businessoffashion.com/articles/news-bites/streetwear-reigns-supreme-say-teens-adidas-gucci

[93] "Luxe Digital Launches to Help Luxury Professionals Connect with Millennial and Generation Z Consumers." prnewswire.com. 19 Jan 2018. https://www.prnewswire.com/news-releases/luxe-digital-launches-to-help-luxury-professionals-con-

nect-with-millennial-and-generation-z-consumers-300585237.html

Inclusivity Movement

[94] West, Samantha. "H&M faced backlash over its 'monkey' sweatshirt ad. It isn't the company's only controversy." washingtonpost.com. 19 Jan 2018. https://www.washingtonpost.com/news/arts-and-entertainment/wp/2018/01/19/hm-faced-backlash-over-its-monkey-sweatshirt-ad-it-isnt-the-companys-only-controversy/?utm_term=.c81b24e56250

[95] Petter, Olivia. "Gucci criticised for putting turbans on white models." independent.co.uk. 23 Feb 2018. https://www.independent.co.uk/life-style/fashion/gucci-white-models-turbans-avan-jogia-fashion-canada-actor-a8224716.html

[96] Dike, Jason. "Why Virgil at Vuitton Only Begins to Combat Industry Racism." Hypebeast.com. 5 Apr 2018. https://hypebeast.com/2018/4/virgil-abloh-louis-vuitton-fashion-diversity-racism

[97] Wilson, Jules. "Black Model Nykhor Paul 'Is Tired of Apologizing for Her Blackness.'" Huffingtonpost.com. 6 Dec 2017. https://www.huffingtonpost.com/2015/07/07/nykhor-paul-white-people-fashion-world-tired-apologizing-blackness_n_7744134.html

[98] Smith, Lydia. "British Vogue: why the new issue is so historic."

independent.co.uk. 10 Nov 2017. https://www.independent.co.uk/news/uk/home-news/british-vogue-new-issue-edward-enninful-december-why-important-explained-a8046906.html

[99] Willingham, AJ. "By 2040, Islam could be the second-largest religion in the US. cnn.com. 10 Jan 2018. https://www.cnn.com/2018/01/10/politics/muslim-population-growth-second-religious-group-trnd/index.html

[100] Diaz, Thatiana. "Revolve Fashion Faces Backlash for Lack of Diversity at Influencer Trip." people.com. 10 Jan 2018. https://people.com/chica/revolve-fashion-faces-backlash-for-lack-of-diversity-at-influencer-trip/

[101] Hargrove, Channing. "#RevolveSoWhite Sparked a Diversity in Fashion Movement on Instagram." refinery29.com. 11 Jan 2018. https://www.refinery29.com/2018/01/187586/valerie-eguavoen-you-belong-now-instagram

Importance of Knowing Your Audience: Diversity in Beauty/Makeup

[102] Dike, Jason. "Why Virgil at Vuitton Only Begins to Combat Industry Racism." Hypebeast.com. 5 Apr 2018. https://hypebeast.com/2018/4/virgil-abloh-louis-vuitton-fashion-diversity-racism

[103] Karimzadeh, Marc. "Victor Glemaud on Diversity, Inspiring

Inclusivity & Being a Black Designer." cfda.com. 20 Feb 2018. https://cfda.com/news/victor-glemaud-on-diversity-inspiring-inclusivity-being-a-black-designer

Part 7: Accessible fashion

[104] Bach, Natasha. "Tommy Hilfiger Has Designed a Fashion Line for People with Disabilities." Fortune.com. 20 Oct 2017.

http://fortune.com/2017/10/20/tommy-hilfiger-disabilities-clothing-line/[105] "Nearly 1 in 5 People Have a Disability in the U.S., Census Bureau Reports." Census.gov. 25 Jul 2012.

https://www.census.gov/newsroom/releases/archives/miscellaneous/cb12-134.html[106] Institute of Medicine. 2007. *The Future of Disability in America.* Washington, DC: The National Academies Press. https://www.nap.edu/catalog/11898/the-future-of-disability-in-america

Activism in Action

[107] Blanks, Tim. "Sinéad Burke Versus The Bell Curve." Businessoffashion.com. 30 Apr 2018.

https://www.businessoffashion.com/articles/people/sinead-burke-versus-the-bell-curve[108] World Report on Disability. http://www.who.int/disabilities/world_report/2011/report/en/

[109] Mama Cax. "Mama Cax on Her Amputation, Beauty, and Body Positivity: 'I Felt Pride, and That Changed Everything." Glamour.com. 3 May 2017.

https://www.glamour.com/story/mama-cax-amputation-beauty-and-body-positivity[110] Brown, Keah. "How Fashion Bramds Can – and Should – Address Shoppers With Disabilities." Glamour.com. 22 Mar 2018. https://www.glamour.com/story/how-fashion-brands-can-address-shoppers-with-disabilities.

[111] Burke, S. (2017, Jun). *Sinéad Burke: Why Design Should Include Everyone."* *https://www.ted.com/talks/sinead_burke_why_design_should_include_everyone*

[112] "The Democratization of Fashion: why consumers come first at NYFW." NOWFASHION. 7 Jul 2018. https://nowfashion.com/the-democratization-of-fashion-why-consumers-come-first-at-nyfw-18651

[113] Adaptawear. https://www.adaptawear.com/

[114] *Customers with Disabilities Mean Business.* U.S. Department of Justice. Jul 2006. https://www.ada.gov/busstat.pd

Accessible fashion at Parsons Open Style Lab

[115] Open Style Lab. http://www.openstylelab.com/

[116] Duan, Noel. "Designing for Disabilities: How Parson's Open Style Lab is Helping to Make Fashion Accessible." Fashionista.com. 27 Sept 2017. https://fashionista.com/2017/09/parsons-open-style-lab-clothing-for-disabilities

[117] "Introducing Comfort Cut." https://www.wolfordshop.com/comfort-cut.html

On the Runway

[118] Foley, Bridget. "Marc Jacobs RTW Spring 2018 ." wwd.com. 13 Sept 2017. https://wwd.com/runway/spring-ready-to-wear-2018/new-york/marc-jacobs/review/

[119] THEFASHIONSPOT. "Report: Fall 2017 Was a Banner Season for Runway Diversity, Especially in New York." thefashionspot.com. 16 Mar 2017. http://www.thefashionspot.com/runway-news/740117-runway-diversity-report-fall-2017/

[120] Richardson, Nikita. "Transgender model Andreja Pejic's inspirational message to 'Vogue' and the world." 22 Apr 2015. https://hellogiggles.com/fashion/andreja-pejic-vogue/

[121] Gregory, Alice. "Has the Fashion Industry Reached a Transgender Turning Point?" vogue.com. 21 Apr 2015. https://www.vogue.com/article/andreja-pejic-transgender-model

[122] Freydkin, Donna. "Is it OK to Joke about Transgender Celebs?" usatoday.com. 14 Jul 2015. https://www.usatoday.com/story/life/tv/2015/07/14/transgender-pop-culture-friends-jazz-jennings-caitlyn-jenner-andreja-pejic/30078787/

[123] Allwood, Emma Hope. "Ivan Bart on the future of modeling." dazeddigital.com. 5 May 2016. http://www.dazeddigital.com/fashion/article/30988/1/img-models-ivan-bart-on-the-future-of-modelling

Part 8: The Changing Face of Leadership

[124] Fernandez, Chantal. "Inside Tory Burch's Entrepreneurship and Empowerment Summit." *The Business of Fashion.* 25 Apr 2018. https://www.businessoffashion.com/articles/news-analysis/inside-tory-burchs-entrepreneurship-and-empowerment-summit

[125] Fernandez, Chantal. "What Makes a Great Fashion CEO?" *The Business of Fashion.* 29 Jan 2018. https://www.businessoffashion.com/articles/professional/what-makes-a-great-fashion-ceo

[126] "Delivering through Diversity." *McKinsey&Company.* Jan 2018. https://www.mckinsey.com/~/media/McKinsey/Business%20Functions/Organization/Our%20Insights/Delivering%20through%20diversity/Delivering-through-diversity_full-report.ashx

[127] Fernandez, Chantal. "Fashion Has a Diversity Problem on the Business Side, Too." *The Business of Fashion.* 2 May 2018. https://www.businessoffashion.com/articles/professional/fashion-has-a-diversity-problem-on-the-business-side-too

[128] Lorenzo, Rocio. "How and Where Diversity Drives Financial Performance." hbr.org. 30 Jan 2018. https://hbr.org/2018/01/how-and-where-diversity-drives-financial-performance

[129] Segran, Elizabeth. "Up, up, and Away: the luggage upstart taking on industry giants." fastcompany.com. 2 Jul 2018. https://www.fastcompany.com/40590583/up-up-and-away-the-luggage-upstart-taking-on-industry-giants

Ethnically ambiguous

[130] Clark, Jessica. "Selling Ethnic Ambiguity." modelalliance.org. http://modelalliance.org/2012/selling-ethnic-ambiguity/selling-ethnic-ambiguity

Know your Market

[131] Finkelstein, Elaina. "New Condé Nast 'Them' website sparks controversy after launch." wjla.com. 1 Nov 2017. https://wjla.com/news/offbeat/new-cond-nast-them-website-sparks-controversy-after-launch

[132] Moylan, Melissa. Personal interview. 1 Mar 2018.

Changes in Fashion Imagery

[133] American Eagle. "Introducing CANdid: Meet Tyler Mitchell." *YouTube*, YouTube, 28 Feb. 2017, www.youtube.com/watch?v=x-IvxowuemNY.

[134] Cascone, Sarah. "Meet Tyler Mitchell, the 23-Year-Old Who Will Be the First Black Photographer to Shoot a 'Vogue' Cover - Thanks to Beyoncé." news.artnet.com. 31 Jul 2018. https://news.artnet.com/art-world/tyler-mitchell-beyonce-vogue-1326308

[135] "The BoF Podcast: Inside the Future of Fashion Image Making with Nick Knight." *The Business of Fashion*. 16 Mar 2018. https://www.businessoffashion.com/articles/podcasts/the-bof-podcast-inside-the-future-of-fashion-image-making-with-nick-knight

[136] Constine, Josh. "Instagram launches IGTV app for creators, 1-hour video uploads." techcrunch.com. 20 Jun 2018. https://techcrunch.com/2018/06/20/igtv/

Part 9: Shifting beauty standards

[137] Rizer Mehran, Maggie. Personal interview. 23 Feb 2018.

Changing beauty standards for young women

- self-improvement

[138] Hess, Amanda. "'I Feel Pretty' and the rise of beauty standard denialism." nytimes.com. 23 Apr 2018. https://www.nytimes.com/2018/04/23/movies/i-feel-pretty-amy-schumer-beauty.html

Part 10: Fashion as empowerment

Halima Aden

[139] Pithers, Ellie. "Halima Aden, The First Hijabi Model on the Cover of Vogue." *The Business of Fashion.* 19 Apr 2018. https://www.vogue.co.uk/article/halima-aden-interview-2018

Girl empowerment at Voices 2017

[140] Doyle, Megan. "How Fashion can Empower Girls." *The Business of Fashion.* 8 Mar 2018. https://www.businessoffashion.com/articles/voices/bof-needs-your-voice-to-empower-girls

[141] "13 reasons why girls are not in school on International Day of the Girl Child." *Theirworld.* 11 Oct 2017. https://reliefweb.int/report/world/13-reasons-why-girls-are-not-school-international-day-girl-child

Women @Dior

[142] "Women @Dior: A Mentorship Programme Empowering Young Women." *The Business of Fashion.* 23 Jul 2017. https://www.businessoffashion.com/articles/video/womendior-a-mentorship-programme-empowering-young-women

Tai Beauchamp

[143] Beauchamp, Tai. Personal interview. 20 Feb 2018.

Leandra Medine, Man Repeller

[144] Pike, Naomi. "Career girl: Leandra Medine." vogue.co.uk. 27 Oct 2017. https://www.vogue.co.uk/article/leandra-medine-man-repeller-business-interview

[145] Medine, Leandra. "A Conversation with Bozoma Saint John." Monocycle. https://www.manrepeller.com/2017/12/monocycle-episode-62-a-conversation-with-bozoma-saint-john.html

LoJo Bands

[146] Fawzi, Laura. Greenzaid, Julia. Personal interview. 8 Mar 2018.

Gucci

[147] Doyle, Megan. "How Fashion can Empower Girls." *The Busi-*

ness of Fashion. 8 Mar 2018. https://www.businessoffashion.com/articles/voices/bof-needs-your-voice-to-empower-girls

Brand Personalization

[148] Garcia, Krista. "The Relentless Pressure to Discount." retail.emarketer.com. 1 May 2018. https://retail.emarketer.com/article/relentless-pressure-discount/5ae766b9ebd40003a0c24672

Customer service/personalization: Piazza Sempione

[149] LaMorte, Gina. "Spring Fashion Trends. Grand Court, The Mall at Short Hills. 5 May 2018.

[150] Hoyos, Karina. Personal interview. 20 May 2018.

[151] O'Connor, Tamison. "Cracking Luxury's Customisation Challenge. *The Business of Fashion.* 20 Feb 2018. https://www.businessoffashion.com/articles/professional/cracking-luxurys-customisation-challenge

Stitch Fix

[152] Lake, Katrina. "Stitch Fix's CEO on Selling Personal Style to the Mass Market." hbr.org. 1 May 2018. https://hbr.org/product/stitch-fix-s-ceo-on-selling-personal-style-to-the-mass-market/R1803A-HCB-ENG?referral=03069

Laura Lee

[153] Williams, Laura Lee. Personal interview. 13 Feb 2018.

Olivia Manduca: Wonderful Wraps and a Lifelong Love for Fashion

[154] Manduca, Olivia. Personal interview. 24 Jan 2018.

Lisa Gorlitsky Schafen

[155] Gorlitsky Schafen, Lisa. Personal interview. 3 Feb 2018.

[156] Taylor, Jonah Levi. "Height, Age, and Measurement Requirements of Modeling." modelingwisdom.com. http://modelingwisdom.com/height-age-and-measurement-requirements-of-modeling

[157] Laurance, Jeremy. "Why our feet are getting bigger." independent.co.uk. 3 Jun 2014. https://www.independent.co.uk/life-style/health-and-families/features/why-our-feet-are-getting-bigger-9481529.html

Customization: Smathers and Branson

[158] Sonsev, Veronika. "Retail Technology and Marketing Trends on the Rise for 2018." forbes.com. 22 Jan 2018. https://www.

forbes.com/sites/veronikasonsev/2018/01/22/retail-technology-and-marketing-trends-on-the-rise-for-2018/#13d2332e64c0

[159] Carter, Peter. Personal interview. 14 Jul 2018.

[160] Smathers&Branson. https://smathersandbranson.com/?gclid=CjwKCAjwwJrbBRAoEiwAGA1B_anTGlINTGVUZZobMLQ557uSizsrRke7IV5SZp9rBn7-slBKfgTkZRoCEtAQAvD_BwE

ACKNOWLEDGEMENTS

Writing this book has been without a doubt the most rewarding project I've ever undertaken. Not only did I learn a lot this past year about the cultural trends changing fashion, but I also learned the importance of growing and cultivating a strong network of mentors and friends. I would like to thank everyone who has been a part of this process and contributed in some way to the final product:

- I thank God for the gift of life.
- I am forever grateful for the doctors who saved my life on May 30, 2017. Thank you for giving me the incredible chance to live and breathe another day. Because of you I have had the opportunity to pursue this passion, so thank you for making that possible.
- My family, who has wholeheartedly supported me in every

endeavor, especially over this past year. I have accomplished more in this year than in any other because of your unceasing love and support. Thank you Mom, Dad, Charlie, and Bridget for pushing me to work hard even on days I really don't feel like it. I love you.

- Special thanks to every therapist I have had the pleasure to work with, particularly Todd Williams and Dave O'Brien. You have no idea how much your commitment and investment in my recovery means to me. This book is for you.

Thank you to all those who helped me in writing this book—everyone I interviewed and had the pleasure to connect with, and the friends who supported me every step of the way. Most notably:

- Greg Nance, thank you for changing my outlook by showing me that every moment of life presents us with a unique set circumstances and choices, and how we choose to address them ultimately influences our outcomes
- Dick Schmitt, thanks for your support and for always looking out for me.
- Shadee Brooks, whose courage and strength inspires me every single day. Duke, you are the reason I wake up in the morning with the strength to try.
- Itay Arad, Alex Batdorf, Brian Bies, Amanda Brown, Christine Butchko, Peter Carter, Francisca Johanek, David Hergenro-eder, Juliette Leader, Peter Malachi, Olivia Manduca, Catherine

Wachtell: thank you for reading my manuscript drafts. I hope you like this version a lot better.

- Thank you to my friends who (literally) stood by my side during hard times.
- And lastly, Eric Koester, thank you for pushing me to make the most of a terrible situation and turn a bad experience into the best thing that ever happened to me.

Made in the USA
Middletown, DE
27 September 2018